ARTIFICIAL INTELLIGENCE

COLLECTION

# INFORMATION ARCHITECTURE

Prof. Marcão Marcus Vinicius Pinto

Disclaimer.

Please note that the information contained in this document is for educational and entertainment purposes only. Every effort has been made to provide complete, accurate, up-to-date, and reliable information. No warranty of any kind is express or implied.

By reading this text, the reader agrees that under no circumstances is the author liable for any losses, direct or indirect, incurred as a result of the use of the information contained in this book, including, but not limited to, errors, omissions, or inaccuracies.

ISBN: 9798340975638

Publishing imprint: Independently published

# Summary

# Welcome!

We live in an era in which information, once just a tool for communication and recording, has become the basis on which our entire digital and technological world rests.

We are at a turning point in human history, where Artificial Intelligence (AI) not only reorganizes our economic and social processes but redefines the meaning of knowledge.

The book you have in your hands, "Information Architecture", is part of a collection entitled "Artificial Intelligence", available on Amazon. This collection seeks to demystify the concepts and tools behind AI, providing a solid foundation for professionals who want to master this transformative technology.

The "Artificial Intelligence" collection is an effort to bring together and systematize the vast and complex field of AI by providing an accessible and practical source of knowledge.

The series is designed to serve both professionals who are already familiar with the AI universe, as well as those who are starting their journeys and seeking a deeper understanding.

Each volume focuses on a crucial aspect of artificial intelligence, from technical fundamentals to ethical considerations and practical challenges. The main objective is to enable readers to navigate, with confidence and competence, the multiple layers that make up this vast and dynamic field.

This book is specially designed for an audience that seeks more than simple theories about AI.

It is intended to:

- Information Technology Professionals: Data engineers, data scientists, software developers, and analysts who need to understand information structures to build robust and efficient solutions.

- Managers and Business Leaders: Executives who want to understand how information architecture can impact on their operations, optimize processes, and generate strategic value for their organizations.

- Students and Researchers: Those who are diving into the fields of computer science and AI looking for a detailed and practical understanding of how information flows and is structured in intelligent systems.

- AI entrepreneurs: Professionals interested in creating and selling AI-based products, who need a solid foundation in data management and creating appropriate information architectures.

These groups of professionals have in common the search for practical and applicable insights, which go beyond theories and enter the concrete reality of how data is transformed into information, and how this information becomes the essence of the knowledge that feeds AI.

To understand the core of Artificial Intelligence, it is essential to understand that data is the essence of everything.

As with any human endeavor, AI is only effective to the extent that the data it processes is structured, reliable, and meaningful.

In this context, Information Architecture emerges as the backbone that supports the entire AI system.

Raw data itself has no value without organization, context and meaning. Information architecture provides the tools to make sense of this universe of data. Without clear and efficient structuring, the full potential of AI can be wasted.

Information, then, becomes the bridge that connects raw data to knowledge, which, in turn, enables AI systems to learn, evolve, and make autonomous decisions.

This book makes that connection by exploring how data is collected, structured, processed, and ultimately transformed into usable knowledge.

Throughout the chapters, practical examples of how this happens in various sectors are presented — from recommendation systems to the use of AI in health and education.

The reader will be guided through fundamental concepts, such as data standardization, semantic modeling, and the integration of information from multiple sources.

To facilitate the understanding of such complex topics, the book includes practical examples taken from real applications. Whether it's a recommendation system that structures user behavior data to suggest new content, or a health system that processes medical data to provide more accurate diagnoses, the idea is for the reader to see how these techniques are applied in the real world.

A striking example is the application of AI in the detection of fake news and misinformation. The book shows how Natural Language Processing (NLP) techniques are used to analyze texts, identify suspicious patterns, and verify the veracity of information.

This example not only illustrates the power of AI but also demonstrates how crucial the right structuring of data is for information integrity.

Understanding information architecture is not just about techniques and methodologies. There are numerous ethical and technical challenges involved in managing large volumes of data.

Issues such as privacy, data security, and algorithmic bias are discussed in depth, providing the reader with critical insight into the responsible use of AI.

The work also highlights the importance of data governance structures, which ensure that the collection and use of information complies with current legislation, such as GDPR and LGPD.

It is through this governance that the trust necessary for AI solutions to thrive in commercial and public environments is established.

As the field of AI continues to evolve, information architecture will become even more crucial. As more data is generated, both in volume and variety, the need for a robust and adaptable framework grows exponentially.

Emerging technologies, such as explainable AI and deep learning, will increasingly rely on well-structured data and accessible information.

This book is not just a technical guide. It is an invitation for you, the reader, to embark on the journey of professional and personal transformation that artificial intelligence can provide.

The complexity and breadth of this field is challenging, but also exciting. By mastering the fundamentals of Information Architecture, you will be positioned to be part of a revolution that is already shaping the future.

Get ready to immerse yourself in a world where data, information, and knowledge are not just components of systems, but the true driving forces of innovation and human progress.

I wish you good reading, good learning and good projects.

Prof. Marcão - Marcus Vinícius Pinto

M.Sc. in Information Technology
Specialist in Information Technology.
Consultant, Mentor and Speaker on Artificial Intelligence,
Information Architecture and Data Governance.
Founder, CEO, teacher and
pedagogical advisor at MVP Consult.

# 1 From Philosophy to Practice: The Essence of Information Management in the Age of Artificial Intelligence.

Artificial intelligence (AI), as a discipline and technology, is the result of a long intellectual and practical journey that dates back to the first attempts to understand and replicate human thought through machines.

At the heart of this journey is information management — the cornerstone that allows AI to not only exist, but also thrive in an increasingly digitized and interconnected world.

## 1.1 The philosophical roots of artificial intelligence.

The idea that machines could, at some level, simulate or replicate human thought is not new.

From Plato's dialogues, where he explores the ideas of knowledge and perception, to Thomas Hobbes' "Leviathan," which suggested that human thought could be reduced to "calculation," the concept of artificial intelligence has deep philosophical roots.

However, it was with the advancement of formal logic in the early twentieth century, especially with the works of Kurt Gödel and Alan Turing, that these ideas began to take shape into technical concepts.

Alan Turing, in his seminal 1950 paper, "Computing Machinery and Intelligence," introduced what we now know as the "Turing Test," a proposed criterion for determining whether a machine can be considered intelligent.

Turing argued that if a machine could trick a human into believing that it was interacting with another human, then that machine could be considered intelligent.

This philosophical framework was instrumental in shaping future discussions about AI, placing an emphasis on language and information processing as the main criteria for intelligence.

From this philosophical foundation comes the understanding that in order for a machine to be able to "think" or act intelligently, it must be able to process information in a similar way to a human.

This leads to the need to develop systems that can collect, store, process, and utilize information efficiently and effectively — which brings us to the crucial role of information management in AI.

1.2    The historical evolution of information management in AI.

Information management, as a field of study, has evolved over the decades in response to advances in data processing capacity and the increasing complexity of AI systems. In the early days of computing, the focus was on developing methods to store and retrieve information efficiently.

With the development of the first relational databases in the 1970s, such as the model proposed by Edgar F. Codd, a more structured understanding of how data could be organized and managed began to emerge.

In the 1980s, with the rise of symbolic artificial intelligence and expert systems, information management began to focus on how to represent knowledge in ways that could be easily processed by machines.

This included the development of ontologies and knowledge representation systems, which sought to capture the semantics and structure of information in such a way that AI systems could use it to reason and make decisions.

With the explosion of Big Data in the early twenty-first century, AI information management has faced new challenges. The amount of data available has grown exponentially, driven by the advent of the internet, social networks, and connected devices.

This has brought to the fore the need for new approaches to store, process, and analyze large volumes of data efficiently.

Technologies such as Hadoop and Spark have emerged to meet these demands, allowing data to be processed in parallel across large clusters of computers.

More recently, the advent of machine learning, particularly deep neural networks, has again transformed information management in AI.

These models require huge amounts of data for training and are extremely sensitive to the quality and structure of the data they receive. This has led to a new emphasis on data curation, where data preparation, cleansing, and organization have become crucial aspects to the success of AI systems.

## 1.3    Machine learning: fundamentals and approaches.

Machine Learning (ML), a subfield of AI, is the process by which AI systems "learn" from data, adjusting its parameters to improve performance on specific tasks.

There are several approaches to machine learning, each with its own characteristics and applications:

1.  Supervised Learning.

    In this approach, AI models are trained with labeled data, where the correct answer is known.

    The goal is to allow the model to learn how to map inputs to correct outputs. A classic example is image classification, where the model is trained to recognize objects in images based on labeled examples.

    Tools such as TensorFlow and PyTorch have been instrumental in the development of supervised learning models.

2.  Unsupervised Learning.

    Unlike supervised learning, unsupervised learning does not utilize labeled data.

    Instead, the model tries to find underlying patterns or structures in the data. A common example is cluster analysis, where the model groups similar data together without having prior information about the categories.

    Algorithms such as K-means and PCA (Principal Component Analysis) are often used in unsupervised learning.

3.  Reinforcement Learning.

This approach involves training models to make decisions in an environment, receiving feedback in the form of rewards or penalties based on the actions taken.

This technique has been widely used in games and robotics, where the goal is to learn optimal strategies through interaction with the environment.

DeepMind's AlphaGo, which beat human champions in the game of Go, is a notable example of reinforcement learning.

4. Artificial Neural Networks.

   Artificial neural networks, inspired by the structure of the human brain, are composed of layers of artificial neurons that process information in a hierarchical manner.

   They are particularly powerful in supervised learning and have been the foundation for many recent advances in AI, especially in computer vision and natural language processing tasks.

1.4    The central role of information management in contemporary AI.

In each of these approaches, information management plays a central role.

The effectiveness of a machine learning model directly depends on the quality, quantity, and relevance of the data it receives.

For example, in supervised learning, mislabeled or insufficient data can lead to a model that does not generalize well to new data, resulting in inaccurate or useless predictions. This places a significant emphasis on the need for data curation, where careful preparation of the data becomes just as important as the algorithm itself.

In addition, information management is crucial for the explainability and transparency of AI systems, topics that have gained increasing attention in contemporary literature.

With the increasing use of AI in critical industries such as healthcare, finance, and security, there is a growing demand for AI systems to be able to explain their decisions in a way that is understandable to humans. This requires that the information used by the models is well-structured and accessible, allowing for effective audits and reviews.

1.5     Interconnection and intertextuality: contributions and theoretical perspectives.

The evolution of information management in AI has not occurred in a vacuum. Over the decades, theorists and researchers from diverse disciplines have contributed to the development of this field.

Claude Shannon, with his theory of information, laid the groundwork for understanding how information can be quantified and transmitted efficiently. His work, "A Mathematical Theory of Communication" (1948), continues to influence the way data is processed and managed in AI systems.

Similarly, John von Neumann's work in computer architecture and cybernetics has profoundly influenced how AI systems process information.

The von Neumann architecture, which organizes the CPU, memory, and I/O into a linear system, is the basis of most modern computers, including those used for AI.

More recently, work by Geoffrey Hinton and Yann LeCun on artificial neural networks and deep learning has transformed the way information is managed in AI.

His research on backpropagation and convolution has revolutionized computer vision and natural language processing, areas that rely heavily on large volumes of efficiently structured and processed data.

## 1.6    Practical applications and contemporary examples.

The impact of information management on AI is evident in a number of practical applications. In healthcare, for example, AI is used to analyze large volumes of medical data, including radiological images, electronic medical records, and genomic data, to help diagnose and treat diseases.

The quality of the data used in these systems is crucial, as wrong decisions can have serious consequences for patients.

In finance, AI is applied to predict market movements, detect fraud, and personalize services for customers. Here, data curation and quality analysis are essential to ensure that forecasts are accurate and that systems can react quickly to new information.

In education, AI systems are used to personalize learning according to the individual needs of students, adjusting the content and pace of instruction based on data on student performance and preferences.

In this context, effective information management is vital to ensure that data on student progress is correctly collected, stored, and analyzed, allowing for timely and effective educational interventions.

Another relevant example is the use of AI in public safety, where intelligent systems analyze vast amounts of data from surveillance cameras, social media, and other sources to predict and prevent crime.

Information management, in this case, involves not only collecting and processing large volumes of data in real time, but also ensuring that this data is used ethically and in compliance with privacy regulations.

1.7    Ethical and technical challenges in information management for AI.

As AI applications become more widespread and influential, the ethical and technical challenges associated with information management gain greater relevance.

One of the main challenges is bias in data, which can result in unfair or discriminatory decisions when AI models are trained on unrepresentative or biased datasets.

Studies, such as those conducted by Joy Buolamwini and Timnit Gebru, have shown how biases present in training data can lead to significant flaws in facial recognition systems, especially with regard to identifying darker-skinned people.

Another critical challenge is data privacy.

With the increasing amount of personal data being collected and processed by AI systems, ensuring that this data is protected from unauthorized access and privacy breaches is of utmost importance.

*This is particularly relevant in industries such as healthcare and finance, where individuals' sensitive data is at stake.*

In addition, the explainability and transparency of AI systems have become central themes in discussions about the future of technology.

As AI models become more complex, understanding and explaining how they arrive at certain decisions becomes a significant technical challenge.

Information management plays a crucial role in this regard, as the clarity and organization of the data used by models is key to ensuring that decisions can be audited and understood by humans.

## 1.8    The future of information management in AI.

The field of information management in AI continues to evolve rapidly, driven by technological advancements and society's growing demands for smarter, safer, and more ethical AI systems.

The future is likely to see the development of new techniques and tools to address current challenges, such as the use of explainable artificial intelligence (XAI), which aims to make AI systems more transparent and understandable to users.

Another promising area is federated learning, an approach that allows AI models to be trained on decentralized data while preserving the privacy of users' data. This can be particularly useful in industries such as healthcare and finance, where privacy is a primary concern.

Additionally, the integration of AI with blockchain is emerging as a potential solution to ensure the integrity and transparency of data used by AI systems.

The use of blockchain can provide an immutable record of all interactions and decisions made by AI systems, facilitating auditing and accountability.

# 2 Structures, modeling, and the evolution of information.

Data architecture is the foundation on which any artificial intelligence (AI) system is built. The effectiveness and efficiency of an AI system depends to a large extent on the robustness and sophistication of the underlying data architecture.

This chapter dives into the depths of data structures and modeling in AI, exploring how different architectural approaches have shaped the development and application of intelligent systems.

From the evolution of relational databases to the advent of Big Data architectures, through data modeling and the integration of multiple sources, this chapter offers a comprehensive analysis of the pillars that underpin contemporary AI.

## 2.1 The roots of data architecture.

The history of data architecture is closely linked to the development of databases, which, in turn, are fundamental for the storage and retrieval of information in AI systems. In the 1970s, Edgar F.

Codd introduced the relational model of data, which revolutionized the way information was organized and accessed. In his seminal paper "A Relational Model of Data for Large Shared Data Banks" (1970), Codd proposed organizing data into tables that could be interrelated by means of primary and foreign keys.

This approach has significantly simplified the handling of large volumes of data, allowing complex queries efficiently.

Relational databases, such as SQL (Structured Query Language), have quickly become the industry standard, allowing AI systems to store and retrieve data in a structured and efficient manner.

However, with the advent of the internet and the explosion of unstructured data (such as text, images, and videos), the limitations of relational databases began to become evident. This has led to the development of NoSQL databases, which offer greater flexibility in how data is stored and accessed.

NoSQL databases such as MongoDB, Cassandra, and Couchbase allow you to store data in a variety of formats, such as documents, graphs, and key-value pairs, without the rigidity of relational tables.

This flexibility is crucial for AI, where data often does not follow a rigid structure and can be highly variable in terms of format and size.

Additionally, NoSQL databases are designed to scale horizontally, allowing large volumes of data to be distributed across multiple servers, which is essential in Big Data applications.

## 2.2 Big data architectures: Data Lakes, Data Warehouses and the evolution of information.

With the exponential growth of data generated by connected devices, social networks, sensors, and other sources, it has become necessary to develop new approaches to storing and processing these vast amounts of information.

Two key concepts have emerged as answers to this challenge: Data Lakes and Data Warehouses.

Data Warehouses are data storage systems that organize information in a structured way, usually in specific schemes, such as the star or snowflake scheme.

They are optimized for fast and efficient queries and are widely used in business analytics and reporting. However, the need to structure data before storing it can be a limitation in contexts where data is generated in varying formats and needs to be analyzed quickly.

On the other hand, Data Lakes offer a more flexible approach. Instead of requiring data to be structured before storage, Data Lakes allow data to be stored in its raw format, regardless of whether it is structured, semi-structured, or unstructured.

This makes Data Lakes ideal for AI applications, where data can be processed and analyzed in innovative and unpredictable ways. Tools such as Apache Hadoop and Apache Spark have been instrumental in the implementation of Data Lakes, enabling distributed processing of large volumes of data.

The choice between Data Warehouses and Data Lakes depends on the specific needs of the AI application. In many cases, organizations opt for a hybrid approach, using both to take advantage of each.

This combination allows highly structured data to be stored in Data Warehouses for fast and accurate analysis, while unstructured or semi-structured data is stored in Data Lakes for flexible and scalable processing.

2.3    Data modeling in artificial intelligence.

Data modeling is a core aspect of data architecture, involving the creation of abstract representations of the information that will be used by AI systems. Data models provide a framework that guides the storage, retrieval, and manipulation of data, ensuring that it is used effectively and efficiently.

There are several approaches to data modeling in AI, each with its own advantages and challenges:

1.  Entity-Relationship (ER) Modeling: Developed by Peter Chen in 1976, ER modeling is a classic technique used to model data in relational systems.

It involves identifying entities (real-world objects, such as customers or products) and the relationships between them.

This approach is widely used in relational databases, but it can be limited in its ability to handle unstructured or dynamic data.

2. Dimensional Modeling: Often used in Data Warehouses, dimensional modeling organizes data around facts and dimensions, making it easier to perform complex analyses.

   This approach is ideal for business intelligence (BI) applications, where query performance is critical.

3. Graph Modeling: In contexts where data has a highly interconnected structure, such as in social networks or recommender systems, graph modeling offers a powerful solution.

   Graph databases, such as Neo4j, allow for the modeling of complex relationships between entities, facilitating analyses that would be difficult or impossible to perform with traditional models.

4. Semantic Modeling: Semantic modeling is used to represent the meaning of data, usually through ontologies or knowledge networks.

   This approach is critical in AI, especially in natural language processing (NLP), where understanding the context and meaning of words is essential.

   The Semantic Web, proposed by Tim Berners-Lee, is an example of how semantic modeling can be applied to enable machines to understand and use information more intelligently.

2.4    Integration of data from multiple sources: challenges and solutions.

One of the biggest difficulties in data architecture for AI is the integration of data from multiple sources.

In an increasingly connected world, data is generated by a variety of devices and systems, each using different formats, standards, and protocols.

Effective integration of this data is crucial to ensure that AI systems can access and utilize all relevant information in a cohesive manner.

There are several approaches to data integration, each with its own unique challenges and benefits:

1. ETL (Extract, Transform, Load): The ETL process is a traditional approach to data integration, involving extracting data from multiple sources, transforming it into a common format, and loading it into a centralized storage system.

   While effective, the ETL process can be time-consuming and can introduce delays in making data available for analysis.

2. Real-Time Integration: With the advent of applications that require real-time decisions, such as autonomous vehicles or high-frequency trading systems, real-time data integration has become a necessity.

   Tools like Apache Kafka enable real-time data streaming, facilitating the seamless integration of information from multiple sources.

3. APIs and Web Services: In many cases, data needs to be integrated from external systems, such as third-party services or public APIs. The use of APIs allows for real-time and programmatic data integration, but it can introduce external dependencies and latency challenges.

4. Data Virtualization: Data virtualization is an approach that allows data to be accessed and used without the need to physically move or copy it. This technique is especially useful in contexts where data is distributed across multiple geographic locations or legacy systems.

## 2.5 Interconnection between data architecture and AI models.

Data architecture is not an isolated component; it is deeply interconnected with the AI models that rely on this data to operate. The choice of data architecture can directly influence the effectiveness of AI models by determining how quickly they can be trained, the accuracy of their predictions, and how easily they can scale.

For example, in deep learning models, the data architecture must be able to deliver large volumes of data quickly, often in parallel, to feed neural networks.

Additionally, the quality of the data provided to the AI is crucial; Noisy or poorly structured data can lead to models that fail to generalize to new data.

In supervised machine learning applications, the data architecture must support efficient labeling of data, ensuring that each input has the correct answer associated with it. This may involve the use of advanced data curation techniques, where labeling is performed by experts or automated through algorithms.

## 2.6 Examples and tips for implementing data architectures in AI.

In the healthcare industry, AI is being used to analyze medical images, predict disease outbreaks, and personalize treatments. In these cases, data architecture must be able to handle large volumes of high-resolution data (such as X-ray images or MRIs) and ensure that this data is stored and accessed efficiently.

Additionally, integrating data from multiple sources, such as electronic medical records, health sensors, and genomic databases, is critical to providing a holistic view of the patient.

In finance, AI is used to detect fraud, predict market movements, and manage investment portfolios. Here, the data architecture must be able to process real-time data, such as financial transactions and market quotes, and integrate this information with historical data to perform accurate predictions.

In education, AI is being applied to personalize learning and identify the needs of students. The data architecture must support the collection and analysis of student performance data, allowing AI systems to adjust the content and pace of instruction based on the information collected.

## 2.7    Ethical considerations in data architecture for AI.

Finally, any discussion of data architecture in AI would be incomplete without addressing the associated ethical considerations.

The way data is collected, stored, and used raises important questions about privacy, security, and fairness. Ensuring that data is managed ethically is crucial for developing responsible AI systems.

For example, when designing data architecture for an AI system that handles personal information, such as health data, it is critical to implement stringent security measures and compliance with regulations such as GDPR.

Additionally, developers should be aware of the biases that can be introduced into the data and work to mitigate them, ensuring that the AI system is fair and unbiased.

# 3 Classification and structuring of data in the context of artificial intelligence.

Artificial intelligence (AI) is based on data—not just any data, but data organized and structured in ways that allow systems to process, analyze, and eventually learn from it.

Understanding the diverse forms that data can take and how that data is organized is essential to building robust and effective AI architecture.

## 3.1 Typologies of data in artificial intelligence.

Data, the basis of any AI system, can be classified into several typologies, each with its specific characteristics and associated challenges. The three main types of data are: structured data, unstructured data, and semi-structured data.

### 3.1.1 Structured data.

Structured data is organized in a highly organized format, usually in tables that allow for easy indexing and searching. This data follows a fixed schema, such as columns and rows, that clearly describe each data item and its relationships to other data.

Examples:

Relational databases (SQL) where data is stored in tables with predefined columns.

Excel spreadsheets containing financial data, such as income, expenses, and profits, organized into columns and rows.

Features:

Ease of Processing: Due to its rigid structure, structured data can be easily queried and analyzed using standard query languages such as SQL.

Standardization: data follows a standard format, which facilitates interoperability between different systems and applications.

Challenges:

Scalability limitations: While structured databases are easy to manage on smaller volumes, they can face performance challenges when dealing with extremely large volumes of data.

Rigidity: The need for a fixed schema limits flexibility in handling data that doesn't fit neatly into a tabular structure.

3.1.2    Unstructured data.

Unstructured data does not follow a specific format or schema and is not organized into a predefined structure. This data represents most of the information generated today and includes texts, images, videos and audios.

Examples:

Text documents, such as reports or articles, are stored in word processing files.

Digital images and videos stored in formats such as JPEG, PNG, or MP4.

Social media posts, emails, and call recordings.

Features:

Diversity of Formats: Unstructured data can take many different forms, making it flexible and information rich.

Processing Complexity: Due to the lack of structure, extracting useful information from unstructured data is a significant challenge, requiring advanced AI techniques such as natural language processing (NLP) and pattern recognition.

Challenges:

Indexing Difficulty: Without a fixed schema, it is difficult to organize, search, and analyze unstructured data efficiently.

Scalability: The sheer volume and diversity of unstructured data can overwhelm traditional data storage and processing systems.

3.1.3   Semi-structured data

Semi-structured data represents a middle ground between structured and unstructured data. They do not follow a rigid scheme, but they do have some organization that allows for easy interpretation and processing.

Examples:

XML or JSON files, where data is organized in a hierarchical or key-value pair structure.

Server logs that contain structured data in a text format, but with a certain regularity.

Features:

Flexibility: They offer greater flexibility than structured data, allowing new fields to be added without having to modify the existing structure.

Ease of Interpretation: Although it does not have the rigidity of structured data, the presence of some organizations makes semi-structured data easier to process than unstructured data.

Challenges:

Transformation Complexity: Integrating semi-structured data with systems that require a fully structured format can be complex, requiring elaborate transformation processes.

Variation in Structure: Flexibility can lead to variations that make it difficult to analyze and integrate large volumes of data.

3.2     Data structuring in the context of artificial intelligence.

Data structuring is essential to the effectiveness of AI systems, as it defines how data will be stored, accessed, and processed.

The way data is structured can directly affect the speed and accuracy of AI algorithms.

1. Relational models and structuring in tables.

In many AI systems, especially those that deal with structured data, relational models remain fundamental.

Organizing data into related tables by primary and foreign keys allows systems to make quick and accurate queries, extracting valuable information from large data sets.

2. Hierarchical structures and semi-structured data.

In contexts where data needs to be organized into layers or levels, such as in XML or JSON files, hierarchical structures are widely used.

These structures allow you to organize the data in a tree of nested elements, making it easier to navigate and manipulate.

For example, in an AI system that analyzes product data in an e-commerce, a JSON file can contain nested information about product categories, descriptions, pricing, and customer reviews, allowing the system to quickly access the necessary details without the need for a rigid structure.

3. Graphs and relationship networks.

For data that involves complex relationships between different entities, such as in social networks or recommendation systems, graphs are an ideal framework.

Graph models, such as the one used by the Neo4j database, represent data such as nodes (entities) and edges (relationships), allowing AI systems to analyze connections and patterns efficiently.

Graphs are especially useful in machine learning algorithms that require analyzing interactions between individuals, such as identifying influences on a social network or recommending products based on previous user interactions.

3.3    The importance of standardizing data formats.

Standardizing data formats is key to ensuring interoperability between different AI systems.

In a world where data is generated by a multitude of sources and in a myriad of formats, standardization facilitates the integration and exchange of information between different systems.

1. Interoperability and integration.

Interoperability is the ability of different systems to share and utilize information efficiently. In AI, interoperability is crucial to allow different algorithms, systems, and platforms to collaborate, using the same data consistently.

For example, in a healthcare application that uses AI to analyze electronic medical records, standardizing data in formats such as HL7 (Health Level Seven) or FHIR (Fast Healthcare Interoperability Resources) is essential to ensure that data can be easily exchanged between hospitals, laboratories, and other healthcare entities.

2. Ease of processing and analysis.

Standardizing data also facilitates processing and analysis, as it allows AI systems to be developed based on predictable and consistent data formats. This reduces the need for data transformation and minimizes the risk of errors during processing.

In addition, standardization allows data from different sources to be combined and analyzed in a cohesive manner, enhancing the insights that can be gained and improving the accuracy of AI models.

3.4    Challenges of standardization and interoperability.

While standardizing data formats is beneficial, it also presents significant challenges. The diversity of data sources and the rapid evolution of AI technologies mean that it is not always possible to establish standards that are widely accepted and adopted.

1. Resistance to standardization.

Organizations and developers may resist standardization because of the cost and effort required to adapt existing systems to new standards. Additionally, standardization can be seen as a constraint on innovation, limiting developers' flexibility in exploring new data formats and structures.

## 2. Evolution of standards.

Data standards need to evolve to keep up with changing technologies and the needs of AI systems. Maintaining compatibility with older standards while adopting new standards can be a significant technical and logistical challenge.

For example, as new data sources such as IoT (Internet of Things) become more common, existing standards may need to be revised to accommodate new types of data and new processing methods.

## 3.5    Practical examples and contemporary applications.

Data structuring and standardization are essential in a variety of AI applications. Below, we discuss some practical examples that illustrate the importance of these practices.

## 1. AI in healthcare: medical image analysis.

In healthcare, AI is being widely used for the analysis of medical images, such as X-rays, CT scans, and MRIs.

In these cases, data is often stored in standardized formats, such as DICOM (Digital Imaging and Communications in Medicine), which allows for the efficient exchange of medical images between different systems and facilitates automated processing by AI algorithms.

## 2. AI in finance: fraud prevention.

In the financial industry, AI is used to detect fraud patterns in transactions. For this to be effective, it is necessary to integrate data from multiple sources, such as banking transactions, credit history, and user behavior.

Standardizing data makes it easier to detect anomalies in real-time, allowing AI systems to identify fraud with greater accuracy.

3. AI in e-commerce: recommendation systems.

On e-commerce platforms, recommendation systems use large volumes of data about products, user behavior, and purchase history.

Structuring this data into graphs allows AI systems to make personalized recommendations, improving the user experience and increasing conversion rates.

3.6    Additional considerations.

The typology and structuring of data are crucial elements in the information architecture in artificial intelligence. The ability to classify, structure, and standardize data largely determines the effectiveness of AI systems and their ability to generate valuable insights.

As AI technologies continue to evolve, the importance of these practices is only likely to grow, requiring developers, data architects, and data scientists to stay up to date with emerging best practices and standards.

# 4 Techniques and Algorithms for Data Transformation and Analysis.

In the universe of artificial intelligence (AI), information processing is a critical component that directly influences the quality and efficiency of the models developed.

Data processing involves a range of techniques and algorithms aimed at transforming raw data into usable information, ensuring that AI models can extract valuable insights and make accurate decisions.

## 4.1 The importance of data processing in AI.

Data processing is an essential prerequisite for any AI system. Raw data, as collected from diverse sources, often contains noise, inconsistencies, and gaps that can compromise the integrity and accuracy of AI models.

Without proper processing, models can generate incorrect, biased, or ineffective results. Therefore, data processing serves as the foundation on which the entire AI system is built, transforming unstructured and chaotic data into structured information ready to be used by advanced algorithms.

## 4.2 Data Processing Techniques

### 4.2.1 ETL (Extract, Transform, Load).

ETL, which stands for Extract, Transform, Load, is a widely used process for moving data from different sources to a centralized storage system, such as a data warehouse or data lake.

The ETL process is divided into three main steps:

1   Extract: In this step, data is extracted from various sources, which may include databases, legacy systems, log files, APIs, and more. Extraction involves collecting data efficiently and securely, ensuring that all the necessary information is captured.

2   Transform: After extraction, the raw data goes through a series of transformations to become usable. This phase can include data cleansing (deduplication, error correction), normalization (standardization of formats), aggregation (data consolidation), and applying business rules to structure the data according to the specific needs of the AI application.

3   Load: Finally, the transformed data is loaded into the target system. This step involves entering the data into the storage environment, where it will be available for analysis and use by AI models. The loading process must be efficient and scalable, especially in environments that handle large volumes of data.

ETL is crucial for data preparation in AI as it ensures that the data is clean, organized, and ready to be used in analysis and learning processes.

The quality of data after ETL directly impacts the quality of AI models, as dirty or poorly transformed data can lead to inaccurate predictions and poor results.

4.3   Data preprocessing.

Data preprocessing is a step that prepares data to be fed into AI models. The goal is to ensure that the data is in a suitable format, free of inconsistencies and ready to be used by learning algorithms.

Pre-processing includes several sub-steps, each of which plays a vital role in preparing the data.

- Data cleansing: Data cleansing involves removing inconsistent, duplicate, or incomplete data.

  Errors in the data, such as missing values, anomalous values, or typographical errors, are common and need to be addressed to prevent them from compromising the integrity of the model.

  Imputation techniques, which replace missing values with estimates based on other data, are often used.

- Normalization and standardization: Normalization is the process of adjusting data values so that they are within a specific range, usually between 0 and 1, which is particularly useful for algorithms that are sensitive to the scale of the data, such as neural networks.

  Standardization, on the other hand, involves transforming the data so that it has a mean of zero and a standard deviation of one, which is essential for algorithms that assume that the data follows a normal distribution.

- Categorical variable transformation: Often, data contains categorical variables that need to be converted into a numerical format to be used in AI models.

  Techniques such as one-hot encoding or label encoding are widely used to transform categorical variables into a form that can be processed by learning algorithms.

- Dimensionality reduction: In datasets with a large number of variables, dimensionality reduction may be necessary to simplify the model and improve its efficiency. Techniques such as PCA (Principal Component Analysis) are used to reduce the number of variables by identifying the most relevant ones for the problem at hand.

Preprocessing is a critical step that ensures that the data is consistent and usable, preventing issues in the data from compromising the performance of the AI models.

Without proper preprocessing, models can become too complex, take longer to train, and ultimately underperform.

4.4    Data cleansing.

Data cleansing is a sub-step of pre-processing, but its importance is such that it deserves a detailed discussion. Dirty data can result from a variety of sources, including human error, software failures, or problems with data collection.

Data cleansing involves identifying and fixing these issues before the data is fed into AI models.

- Duplicate detection and removal: Duplicate data can skew model results, especially in analyses that rely on accurate hit counting.

  Duplicate detection is done through record matching techniques, which compare different data entries to identify duplicate records.

- Correction of typographical errors and inconsistencies: Typographical errors and inconsistencies in the data, such as different formats for dates or variations in text capitalization, can cause problems during analysis.

Data cleansing involves standardizing these formats and correcting any inconsistencies detected.

- Handling missing data: Missing values can be particularly problematic, as many AI algorithms can't handle missing inputs.

  There are several approaches to dealing with missing data, including imputing values based on means or media, deleting incomplete records, or using more advanced models to predict missing values.

Data cleansing not only improves the accuracy of AI models but also reduces the risk of issues during model training and execution. It is an essential step in ensuring that the data is of high quality and ready for use.

4.5    Normalization of data.

Data normalization is a technique that adjusts data values to a common scale, usually between 0 and 1.

This technique is essential for algorithms that calculate distances or rely on the scale of data, such as neural networks and distance-based learning algorithms (e.g., KNN K-Nearest Neighbors).

- Normalization techniques: Normalization can be performed in a variety of ways, including min-max scaling, which transforms the data so that all values are within a specific range (usually 0 to 1), and z-score normalization, which transforms the data so that it has a mean of 0 and a standard deviation of 1.

- Impact on model quality: Normalization helps prevent large-scale variables from dominating model learning, which can result in suboptimal performance. By ensuring that all data is at a comparable scale, normalization improves the efficiency and accuracy of the model.

- Practical examples: In a recommendation system that uses AI, normalization can ensure that user reviews, which can range from 1 to 5 stars, are treated equitably alongside other variables such as purchase frequency or interaction time.

4.6    Impact of data processing on the quality and efficiency of AI models.

Data processing has a direct and significant impact on the quality and efficiency of AI models. Well-processed and prepared data results in more accurate, efficient, and scalable models.

On the other hand, poorly processed data can lead to models that are not only inaccurate but also require more resources for training and execution.

Accuracy and robustness: Models trained on high-quality data tend to be more accurate and robust, able to generalize well to new data and situations.

The accuracy of the model is often a direct reflection of the quality of the data used during training.

Computational efficiency: proper data processing can also improve the computational efficiency of models. Normalized and reduced dimensionality data requires less processing power, which results in faster training times and lower operating costs.

Reducing bias: Processing techniques such as cleansing and normalization can help reduce bias in the data by ensuring that the AI model is fair and unbiased. This is particularly important in critical applications, such as financial decisions or medical diagnostics, where biases can have serious consequences.

4.7     Challenges and ethical considerations in data processing.

Data processing in AI is not without its ethical challenges and considerations. Issues such as data privacy, transparency in processing methods, and the impact of automated decisions require careful consideration.

- Data privacy and security: The collection and processing of large volumes of data often involves sensitive personal information.

  It is crucial to ensure that this data is protected from unauthorized access and that processing practices comply with regulations such as GDPR.

- Transparency and explainability: As AI models become more complex, transparency in data processing methods is essential to ensure that automated decisions can be understood and explained.

  The lack of transparency can lead to distrust and resistance to the use of AI in critical industries.

- Social impact: The way data is processed can influence the social impact of decisions made by AI models.

  It is important to consider how processing techniques can perpetuate or mitigate inequities, especially in areas such as recruitment, criminal justice, and healthcare.

# 5 Methods to ensure data integrity and reliability.

In the field of artificial intelligence (AI), data quality is a determining factor in the success or failure of any system or model. High-quality data enables AI algorithms to make accurate predictions, make informed decisions, and identify meaningful patterns.

On the other hand, low-quality data can introduce biases, errors, and inefficiencies that compromise the integrity and reliability of the results.

## 5.1 The Importance of Data Quality in Artificial Intelligence.

Data quality is essential in all aspects of AI development, from the training phase to the implementation and maintenance of the models.

Data quality directly impacts the effectiveness of machine learning algorithms and the ability of AI systems to generalize from training data to new cases.

- Prediction accuracy: Models trained with accurate data produce more reliable predictions. In contrast, inaccurate data can lead to models making incorrect assumptions or wrong predictions, directly impacting AI-based decision-making.

- Reduction of biases: the quality of the data also influences the fairness of the model. Biased or incomplete data can perpetuate or even amplify existing biases, resulting in unfair or discriminatory decisions.

- Operational efficiency: High-quality data reduces the need for rework and reprocessing, increasing operational efficiency. Models trained on clean, consistent data require fewer computational resources and time to develop and maintain.

## 5.2    Data quality criteria.

### 5.2.1    Accuracy.

Accuracy refers to the degree to which the data correctly reflect the reality they are intended to represent. Accurate data is essential to ensure that AI models can learn real-world patterns and make predictions that are applicable to the real world.

Example: In an AI system used for medical diagnosis, the accuracy of the data is critical. If the input data, such as test results or reported symptoms, is not accurate, the system can come up with incorrect diagnoses, compromising the health of patients.

Accuracy assurance techniques: Cross-validating data against reliable sources or using data verification methods such as audits and sampling are effective strategies to ensure data accuracy.

### 5.2.2    Completeness.

Data completeness refers to the extent to which all the data necessary for a given purpose is present. Incomplete data can lead to models that fail to capture all aspects of a problem, resulting in flawed or partial predictions.

- Example: In an AI system for credit analysis, a lack of critical information such as credit history or income can lead to inaccurate risk assessments, resulting in poor credit decisions.

- Completeness Assurance Techniques: Missing data imputation, where missing values are filled in based on estimates derived from other data, is a common technique for improving data completeness. Another approach is the integration of multiple data sources to cover gaps.

### 5.2.3    Consistency.

Data consistency refers to the uniformity of data across different records, systems, or databases. Inconsistent data can introduce contradictions that confuse AI algorithms and lead to incorrect conclusions.

- Example: If a customer is registered in different systems of a company with slightly different names (e.g., "John Smith" and "John Smith"), this can lead to duplication or loss of important information.

- Consistency assurance techniques: Applying validation and referential integrity rules can help maintain data consistency. Additionally, the use of data deduplication and normalization tools is critical to correcting inconsistencies.

### 5.2.4    Timeliness.

Data timeliness, or "timeliness," refers to how quickly data is captured and made available for use after the events it records.

Outdated data can lead to decisions that do not reflect current conditions, reducing the effectiveness of the AI model.

- Example: in AI systems that operate in real time, such as those used in stock trading, the timeliness of the data is crucial. Decisions based on outdated data can result in significant financial losses.

- Timeliness Assurance Techniques: Implementing real-time or near-real-time data pipelines, as well as utilizing data streaming technologies such as Apache Kafka, are effective methods for ensuring data timeliness.

5.3    Tools and techniques for evaluating and improving data quality.

Data quality assessment and improvement are ongoing processes that require a combination of specialized tools and well-defined techniques.

Below, we explore some of the key tools and techniques used by data professionals and data scientists to ensure that data is ready for use in AI.

5.3.1    Data quality tools.

- Great expectations: An open-source tool that allows users to define, validate, and document expectations about their data.

  Great Expectations helps ensure that data is consistent with established expectations by providing detailed reports on data quality.

- Talend data quality: a complete solution for data profiling, deduplication, standardization and data validation. Talend allows you to create data quality rules that are automatically applied to data in transit.

- Rifacta Wrangler: A data cleansing and transformation tool that allows users to explore, structure, and clean data in an interactive way. Trifacta is especially useful for preparing large volumes of data for analysis.

5.3.2    Data Quality Assessment Techniques

- Data profiling: Data profiling involves analyzing data in detail to understand its structure, content, and quality.

Data profiling tools can identify patterns, anomalies, and inconsistencies in data, allowing data professionals to take corrective action before using the data in AI models.

- Data audits: Data audits are systematic reviews of data collection, storage, and processing processes to ensure that quality practices are followed.

  Audits can reveal hidden issues in the data, such as biases, input errors, or data capture failures.

- Validation tests: Validation tests apply specific rules to the data to verify its compliance with predefined criteria, such as format, consistency, and range of values.

  Validation tests are particularly useful for ensuring data integrity over time.

5.3.3   Data quality improvement techniques.

- Deduplication: Data deduplication removes duplicate records from a dataset, ensuring that each entity is represented only once. Deduplication tools use record-matching algorithms to identify and remove duplicates.

- Normalization: Data normalization ensures that data adheres to uniform standards of naming, formatting, and structure.

  This is especially important in datasets that come from multiple sources, where inconsistencies can cause problems during processing.

- Imputation of missing data: Imputation involves filling in missing values based on estimates derived from other data. This can be done through simple techniques, such as replacing with mean or median, or through more advanced methods, such as machine learning algorithms.

5.4    Impact of data quality on artificial intelligence.

Data quality directly affects the effectiveness of AI models by influencing the models' ability to learn, generalize, and operate reliably.

- Model accuracy: High-quality data allows AI models to make more accurate and reliable predictions. The accuracy of the data, for example, is directly linked to the accuracy of the model: the more accurate the data, the more accurate the model's predictions will be.

- Generalization: The ability of an AI model to generalize new data is critical to its practical utility. Consistent and complete data helps ensure that the model is able to apply the patterns learned to new data sets.

- Reduction of biases: Biases in data can lead to unfair or discriminatory decisions. Data cleansing and normalization can help mitigate bias, ensuring that the AI model is fair and unbiased.

# 6 Context and semantic modeling for smart data.

The ability of artificial intelligence (AI) to understand and utilize the context of data is one of the most challenging and promising areas in the field of technology.

While the processing of structured and unstructured data has allowed for great advances, it is the understanding of the context and semantics of data that truly differentiates intelligent systems.

## 6.1 The importance of context in AI

Understanding the context is critical for AI to be able to make informed and relevant decisions. Context allows AI systems to understand the nuances of data, recognize implicit relationships, and interpret information in a more human-like way.

Without context, AI systems can provide answers that are technically correct but fail to capture the underlying meaning or intent.

- Practical Example: Consider a virtual assistant such as Siri or Alexa. When a user asks "What is the weather?", context is crucial for the assistant to understand that the user is referring to the weather in the current location.

  Without context, AI could provide irrelevant information, such as weather data from a random location or a past date.

- Impact on Accuracy: The ability to capture and utilize context directly impacts the accuracy and relevance of AI responses. Models that integrate context can provide more accurate predictions, more appropriate recommendations, and more natural interactions.

## 6.2 Semantic modeling in AI.

Semantic modeling refers to the process of structuring data in such a way that its meaning and relationships can be understood and utilized by AI systems.

This involves creating formal representations of knowledge, allowing AI to not only process data but also understand and interpret the underlying meaning.

### 6.2.1   Ontologies.

Ontologies are formal structures that represent knowledge within a specific domain, including the concepts (classes), their properties (attributes), and the relationships between those concepts.

Ontologies play a vital role in semantic modeling, providing a foundation for AI to understand the context and meaning of data.

- Ontology example: Health Ontology (SNOMED CT) is one of the broadest ontologies used in medicine, allowing AI systems to understand and use medical terms in a standardized way. This facilitates interoperability between different healthcare systems and improves the accuracy of diagnoses made by AI systems.

- Ontology construction: Creating an ontology involves identifying the key concepts within a domain, defining the relationships between those concepts, and formalizing that knowledge into a framework that can be used by AI systems. Tools like Protégé are widely used for the construction of ontologies.

### 6.2.2   Knowledge networks.

Knowledge networks are graphical representations that model the interconnection of concepts and entities within a domain, using nodes and edges to represent entities and their relationships, respectively. These networks allow AI to navigate and reason about knowledge in an efficient manner.

- Google Knowledge Graph: A prominent example of a knowledge network is the Google Knowledge Graph, which organizes and links information from multiple sources to provide more complete and contextually relevant answers to user queries.

  When a user searches for a historical figure, for example, the Knowledge Graph not only provides a description, but also relates that figure to events, locations, and other personalities, enriching the understanding of the context.

- Practical Applications: Knowledge networks are used in recommendation systems, where AI needs to understand the relationships between different items to suggest relevant products or services to the user.

  They are also fundamental in virtual assistants, where the context is dynamic and the relationships between different information are critical to the quality of the response.

6.3     Models of semantic representation.

Semantic representation models, such as Word2Vec and BERT (Bidirectional Encoder Representations from Transformers), are techniques that allow AI to understand the meaning of words in relation to their context.

These models capture the semantic relationships between words, allowing the AI to understand nuances such as synonymy, antonymy, and polysemy.

- Word2Vec: developed by Tomas Mikolov in 2013, Word2Vec is a model that represents words as vectors in a multidimensional space, where the proximity between vectors indicates the semantic similarity between words.

  This model has been widely used in natural language processing (NLP) tasks such as sentiment analysis and machine translation.

- BERT: Launched by Google in 2018, BERT is a pre-trained language model that understands the context of words in a sentence by considering the entire sequence of words, rather than just the previous or subsequent word.

  BERT has revolutionized NLP tasks, such as question answering and text classification, by allowing AI to better understand contextual meaning.

## 6.4    Structuring and contextualization of information in AI.

Information structuring refers to the organization of data in such a way that its interpretation and use are optimized for AI systems.

Contextualizing information means sitting in a specific environment or setting, so that its relevance and application are better understood.

### 6.4.1    Contextualization through Metadata.

Metadata is data that describes other data. They provide additional context that helps the AI understand how, when, and by whom the data was created, as well as other information relevant to its interpretation.

- Example of metadata: In a digital image, metadata can include information about the camera used, the geographic location where the photo was taken, and the date and time of capture. This metadata allows the AI to make more accurate inferences about the content of the image.

- Importance of metadata: Metadata is essential for the interoperability of AI systems, as it provides the necessary context for different systems to interpret and utilize data consistently.

6.4.2   Contextualization through Natural Language Processing (NLP).

NLP is a field of AI that deals with the interaction between computers and human language.

Contextualization through NLP involves analyzing text or speech to extract contextual information that helps the AI understand the meaning of words in relation to their use in sentences or conversations.

Sentiment Analysis: NLP is widely used to analyze sentiment in texts, such as social media posts, where context is crucial in determining whether a word is used positively or negatively.

Word Sense Disambiguation: Word Sense Disambiguation is another critical application of NLP, where AI needs to understand the context to identify the correct meaning of a word that has multiple meanings.

6.4.3   Contextualization through neural networks and deep learning.

Deep neural networks (deep learning) have been shown to be highly effective in contextualizing data, especially in tasks involving images, sound, and language.

These networks are able to learn high-level representations of the data, which capture context in a more abstract and powerful way.

- Convolutional Networks (CNNs): In computer vision tasks, CNNs are used to capture spatial context in images, allowing the AI to recognize objects in different positions and under different lighting conditions.

- Recurrent Networks (RNNs): RNNs, including their variants such as LSTMs (Long Short-Term Memory), are used to capture temporal context in sequential data, such as time series or language.

  They are particularly useful in forecasting tasks, where the order of the data is crucial for correct interpretation.

6.5     Challenges in context and semantic modeling.

While context and semantic modeling offers tremendous benefits, it also presents significant challenges, both technical and ethical.

1     Computational complexity.

Semantic modeling and building knowledge networks are computationally intensive tasks, requiring large volumes of data and processing power.

Complexity increases as one tries to capture richer contexts and deeper semantic nuances.

- Scalability challenges: As knowledge networks grow in size and complexity, it becomes challenging to scale them efficiently without sacrificing performance.

2     Ambiguity and variability.

Human language is fraught with ambiguities and contextual variations that are difficult to model.

Words and phrases can have different meanings depending on the context, and capturing these subtleties is a complex task for AI.

- Contextual Disambiguation: Semantic models need to be able to disambiguate words in different contexts, which requires a deep understanding of the language and the specific domain in which they are being applied.

3    Ethical considerations.

Semantic modeling and contextualization of data raise ethical questions, especially regarding privacy and bias. When collecting and modeling contextual data, there is a risk of invasion of privacy and reinforcing existing biases.

- Data privacy: The use of context and metadata can reveal sensitive information that was not explicitly present in the original data, raising concerns about users' privacy.

- Bias mitigation: It is essential that semantic models are trained on diverse data and audited regularly to mitigate biases that may arise from contextual interpretation of data.

6.6    Practical and future applications of context and semantic modeling in AI.

Context and semantic modeling is already being applied in several areas, with significant impacts on how AI interacts with data and makes decisions.

### 6.6.1   Virtual assistants and chatbots.

Virtual assistants, such as Siri, Alexa, and Google Assistant, rely heavily on semantic modeling to understand and respond appropriately to user requests.

The ability to understand the context and meaning of words allows these assistants to provide more accurate and useful answers.

### 6.6.2   Recommendation systems.

Recommendation systems, used on platforms such as Netflix and Amazon, use knowledge networks and semantic modeling to understand user preferences and offer personalized suggestions. By capturing the context of users' previous interactions, these systems can more accurately predict what a user might like.

### 6.6.3   Health and medical diagnosis.

In healthcare, AI is being used to analyze medical records and diagnoses, where understanding the clinical context is key. Semantic models allow AI to interpret symptoms and medical histories in a contextualized way, helping doctors make more informed decisions.

### 6.6.4   Personalized education

Personalized education is another area where context modeling is transforming AI.

Adaptive learning platforms use contextual data about student performance and preferences to adjust content and the pace of instruction, providing a more effective and engaging learning experience.

# 7 Checking fake news and disinformation by AI.

The spread of fake news and misinformation is one of the most critical challenges of the digital age. With the exponential growth of social networks and the ease of sharing information, the impact of fake news can be devastating, affecting everything from political elections to public health issues.

Artificial intelligence (AI) has emerged as a powerful tool to combat this spread, using advanced techniques to identify, classify, and mitigate the spread of misleading content.

## 7.1 The rise of fake news and disinformation.

The term "fake news" refers to deliberately false or misleading information, spread through social media, websites, and other digital platforms, with the intention of manipulating public opinion, generating revenue, or promoting specific agendas.

Disinformation goes further, encompassing the intentional dissemination of inaccurate information, regardless of its form or purpose.

- Social Impact: Fake news has the power to influence electoral decisions, exacerbate social divisions, and even harm public health, as seen during the COVID-19 pandemic, where false information about treatments and vaccines had a significant impact.

- Accelerated Diffusion: Social media platforms facilitate the spread of fake news due to their global reach and speed of sharing, often outpacing the spread of verified information.

AI fake news detection involves applying a variety of machine learning and natural language processing (NLP) techniques to analyze content and identify signs of misinformation.

These techniques are designed to address the complexity and subtlety of fake news, which can range from completely fabricated news to distorted partially true information.

## 7.2    AI techniques for detecting fake news.

### 7.2.1    Text classification.

One of the most common techniques used to detect fake news is text classification, where supervised learning algorithms are trained to distinguish between true and false news based on patterns learned from a labeled dataset.

- Classification models: Models such as Naive Bayes, Support Vector Machines (SVM), and deep neural networks are often used for this task.

  They analyze the text for linguistic patterns, such as the use of exaggerated adjectives, sensationalist words, and grammatical structure that may indicate fake news.

- Practical example: An AI system trained on a large corpus of news articles can identify that a headline with terms such as "shock," "revolution," or "urgent" is more likely to be sensationalist and potentially false.

## 7.2.2 Automated fact-checking.

Automated fact-checking is a technique where AI attempts to corroborate the claims made in an article by comparing them to reliable sources. This process involves extracting key information from the text and comparing it with a database of verified facts.

- NLP and Entity Extraction: NLP techniques are used to identify entities (such as names of people, places, events) and relationships in the text. The AI then checks these entities and their relationships against credible sources to determine the veracity of the claims.

- Practical example: if an article claims that "scientists have discovered a cure for cancer", the AI can search reliable scientific databases to verify that such a discovery was actually made.

## 7.2.3 Detection of manipulated images and videos.

Image and video manipulation is a common disinformation technique, with AI being used to create fake visual content that looks authentic. Detecting these manipulations requires advanced computer vision techniques.

- Deepfakes: One of the most recent challenges is the creation of deepfakes, where generative neural network algorithms, such as GANs (Generative Adversarial Networks), are used to create fake videos of people saying or doing things that never happened.

- Deepfake detection: AI is also used to detect deepfakes by analyzing inconsistencies in aspects such as lighting, shadows, lip movement, and other details that may be difficult to replicate perfectly in fake videos.

### 7.2.4  Social media analysis.

The spread of fake news often occurs on social networks, where bots and fake accounts amplify the reach of misinformation. AI is used to analyze patterns of spread and identify anomalous behavior that suggests a coordinated disinformation campaign.

- Bot detection: Machine learning algorithms are trained to identify automated accounts by analyzing characteristics such as posting frequency, interaction patterns, and language usage, differentiating them from legitimate human users.

- Mapping disinformation networks: AI can also map disinformation networks, tracking how information is shared and identifying clusters of activity that indicate coordinated attempts to spread fake news.

### 7.3  Technical challenges in the detection of fake news.

While AI has made significant strides in detecting fake news, it still faces several technical challenges that limit its effectiveness.

### 7.3.1  Ambiguity and subjectivity.

Many fake news stories contain true elements mixed with misleading information, making the task of detection extremely difficult. Subjectivity in the interpretation of the text can also make it difficult to determine a piece of news as false.

- Contextualization Challenges: Understanding context is crucial, as a statement that is true in one context may be false in another. AI still struggles to pick up on these nuances effectively.

### 7.3.2   Evasion and adaptation of disinformers.

Fake news creators are continually adapting their techniques to fool detection systems, using strategies such as changing keywords, using metaphors or irony, and manipulating context.

- Model adaptation: AI must be continuously updated and trained on new types of data to keep up with the ever-evolving tactics of disinformers.

### 7.3.3   Bias in detection models.

AI models can introduce or amplify biases, especially if they are trained on datasets that are not representative. This can lead to failures in detecting fake news in different languages, cultures, or contexts.

- Generalization challenges: Ensuring that AI models work effectively in diverse contexts is an ongoing challenge, requiring training on a wide range of data and scenarios.

### 7.4   Ethical challenges in the detection of fake news.

In addition to the technical challenges, AI detection of fake news raises significant ethical questions.

### 7.4.1   Freedom of expression.

There is a fine line between the detection of fake news and censorship. AI systems that are too strict in identifying false content can end up silencing legitimate opinions or critical debates, affecting freedom of expression.

- Balancing Challenges: Platforms need to balance the need to curb misinformation with protecting freedom of expression, avoiding censorship of content that may be controversial but not necessarily false.

### 7.4.2   Transparency and accountability.

Transparency in the criteria and algorithms used to detect fake news is crucial to ensure public trust. However, the complexity of AI models can make it difficult to explain detection decisions.

- Explainability challenges: AI models often operate as "black boxes," where decisions are difficult to interpret. This can lead to concerns about accountability and the potential lack of transparency in content moderation processes.

### 7.4.3   Political implications.

The detection of fake news also has political implications, especially when it involves content that influences elections or government issues. AI can be seen as a tool of control, and the way it is used can have significant consequences for democracy.

Manipulation risks: There is a risk that governments or other entities will use AI systems to manipulate public opinion by labeling truthful content as false to suppress unwanted information.

### 7.5   Current limitations of fake news detection technologies.

Despite the advances, fake news detection technologies still face significant limitations.

1.  Reliance on trained data.

    The effectiveness of AI models depends on the quality and comprehensiveness of the data on which they are trained. Models trained on limited or biased data may not be able to generalize to new types of fake news or different cultural contexts.

2.  Speed of dissemination vs. speed of detection.

    Fake news spreads quickly, often before AI systems

    have the chance to identify and mitigate them. The time it takes to verify and classify content as false may be insufficient to contain its viral spread.

3.  Complexity in contextual understanding.

    AI models still struggle to understand the broader context in which a news story was written, including cultural references and linguistic nuances that are essential for determining the veracity of a piece of information.

7.6     Future of AI in the fight against fake news.

The future of combating fake news with AI involves the development of more advanced and integrated technologies, as well as collaboration between technology companies, governments, and civil society.

4.  Integration of multiple data sources

    The use of multiple data sources, including metadata and post history, can improve the accuracy of detection systems. AI will be able to integrate different types of information to provide a more robust assessment of the veracity of a piece of content.

5.  Improved model explainability.

    Developing AI models that can clearly explain how they arrived at a given detection decision will help increase trust and transparency, making it easier for the public to accept these technologies.

6.  Education and media literacy

    In addition to technology, it is essential to invest in media literacy and education, empowering people to recognize and combat misinformation for themselves. AI can complement these efforts, but public awareness is a vital component in the fight against fake news.

# 8 Protection of sensitive information and regulatory compliance.

Data privacy and security are central issues in the development and application of artificial intelligence (AI) systems. With the increasing use of AI in various areas, from healthcare to finance, the protection of sensitive information has become a crucial priority.

This chapter explores the best practices and challenges involved in data protection in AI, as well as analyzing the impact of regulations such as the GDPR (General Data Protection Regulation) and the LGPD (General Data Protection Law) on information management in AI.

Through this discussion, we highlight the need for a balance between technological innovation and the guarantee of the fundamental rights to privacy and security of individuals.

Data protection is critical in a world where AI plays an increasingly central role in decision-making and the processing of large volumes of personal information. AI systems frequently handle highly sensitive data such as health information, financial data, and browsing histories, making the privacy and security of that data a primary concern.

- Risks associated with the use of AI: The use of AI without proper safeguards can lead to privacy breaches, misuse of data, and even mishandling of information. Additionally, unauthorized access to sensitive data can have serious consequences, both for individuals and organizations.

- Need for protection: Protecting data is essential not only to comply with legal regulations, but also to maintain user trust and ensure that AI is used ethically and responsibly.

## 8.1 Challenges in data protection in AI.

### 8.1.1 Volume and variety of data.

AI systems operate with large volumes of data, coming from various sources. The diversity and volume of data increases the complexity of protecting this information, especially when data is collected and stored in different locations or systems.

- Storage and processing challenges: Ensuring the security of large volumes of data distributed across multiple servers and geographic locations requires a robust infrastructure, with advanced encryption and access control mechanisms.

- Integration issues: Integrating data from different sources, such as legacy systems and new technologies, can introduce vulnerabilities that are exploitable by malicious actors.

### 8.1.2 Anonymization and pseudonymization of data.

Anonymizing or pseudonymizing data is a common practice to protect the privacy of individuals while maintaining the usefulness of the data for AI analysis. However, these techniques are not foolproof and present significant challenges.

- Incomplete anonymization: Anonymization can be reversed, especially when combined with other data sources, allowing identities to be reconstituted. This raises concerns about the effectiveness of anonymization as a privacy-protecting tool.

- Risk of re-identification: Even with pseudonymization, where direct identifiers are replaced by pseudonyms, there is a risk of re-identification through the correlation of seemingly harmless data.

### 8.1.3   Security in algorithms and models.

The AI algorithms and models themselves can be targets of attacks, such as model inversion or adversarial attacks, where intruders attempt to manipulate the model to reveal sensitive information or cause malfunctions.

- Adversarial attacks: Such attacks involve introducing small perturbations into the input data that trick the AI model into making wrong predictions or revealing sensitive information.

- Protecting models: Protecting AI models from such attacks requires the implementation of advanced security techniques, such as robust learning and continuous model validation.

### 8.2   Data Protection Regulations.

With the growing awareness of the risks associated with data privacy, several regulations have been implemented globally to protect individuals' data and ensure that organizations follow safe and transparent practices in the use of AI.

### 8.3   GDPR (General Data Protection Regulation).

The GDPR, implemented in the European Union in 2018, is one of the most comprehensive and influential data protection regulations. It sets out strict guidelines on how personal data should be collected, stored, and used, including specific provisions for AI.

- Consent and Transparency: The GDPR requires organizations to obtain explicit consent from individuals before collecting and processing their data. Additionally, organizations must be transparent about how data will be used, including the application of AI.

- Right to Be Forgotten: Individuals have the right to request the deletion of their personal data, a technical challenge for AI systems that store and process large volumes of historical data.

- Impact on AI Development: The GDPR imposes restrictions on the use of personal data in AI, especially regarding automated decisions such as credit profiles or employment decisions, requiring organizations to implement safeguards to protect the rights of individuals.

## 8.4    LGPD (General Data Protection Law).

The LGPD, implemented in Brazil in 2020, follows many of the principles established by the GDPR, but with some adaptations to the local context. The LGPD regulates the use of personal data, imposing similar obligations in terms of consent, transparency, and security.

- Legal Bases for Processing: The LGPD defines several legal bases under which data may be processed, including explicit consent and the protection of life. This requires organizations to clearly justify the use of AI based on these criteria.

- Data subject rights: The LGPD gives individuals the right to access, correct, and delete their personal data, which presents challenges for practical implementation in AI systems.

- Sanctions and consequences: The LGPD provides for significant sanctions for violations, including fines and the suspension of data use, encouraging organizations to implement stringent security measures in their AI systems.

## 8.5 Best practices for data protection in AI.

Ensuring data privacy and security in AI requires a multifaceted approach, which combines advanced technology with robust organizational policies. Below, we highlight some of the best practices for protecting data used in AI.

### 8.5.1 Data encryption.

Encryption is one of the most effective techniques for protecting data, both in transit and at rest. Encryption ensures that even if data is intercepted, it cannot be read or used without the decryption key.

- Encryption in transit and at rest: Implementing encryption during data transfer and while data is stored on servers is critical to protecting sensitive information.

- Encryption of sensitive data: Highly sensitive data, such as health and financial information, must be encrypted with robust techniques, such as end-to-end encryption, to ensure that only authorized users can access it.

### 8.5.2 Access control and authentication.

Strict access control and authentication are essential to ensure that only authorized users can access sensitive data.

- Multi-factor authentication: Implementing multi-factor authentication (MFA) helps prevent unauthorized access, even if a password is compromised.

- Access privileges: Restrict access to data based on need, ensuring that only the people who really need the information can access it.

### 8.5.3 Audits and continuous monitoring.

Regular audits and continuous monitoring of data usage help identify and mitigate security risks before they can cause damage.

- Access monitoring: Implementing monitoring systems to track who accesses data, when, and for what purpose, ensuring that any suspicious activity is detected quickly.

- Regular audits: Conduct regular audits of data security processes to ensure that all practices are compliant with applicable regulations and best practices.

### 8.5.4 Training and awareness.

Data security is only as strong as the people who protect it. Training and awareness are essential to ensure that everyone involved in the development and operation of AI systems understands the importance of data security and follows best practices.

- Ongoing education: Provide ongoing training on data security and privacy, with a focus on new threats and emerging best practices.

- Security culture: promoting an organizational culture that values privacy and security, encouraging all employees to take responsibility for data protection.

### 8.6 Impact of regulations on AI innovation.

While regulations such as GDPR and LGPD are essential for protecting the privacy of individuals, they also pose significant challenges for AI innovation.

1. Balance between compliance and innovation.

Regulations require organizations to be meticulous in protecting data, which can restrict agility and innovation in AI projects. However, compliance with these regulations can also create opportunities for responsible and ethical innovation.

- Responsible Innovation: Companies that can balance innovation with compliance can create AI solutions that are both effective and ethical, building trust with their users and customers.

2. Compliance costs.

Implementing the necessary measures to comply with regulations such as GDPR and LGPD can be costly and time-consuming, especially for small and medium-sized businesses.

- Investment Required: Businesses need to invest in security infrastructure, training, and legal advice to ensure compliance, which can pose a significant financial challenge.

3. Improvement of data protection practices.

Despite the challenges, regulations have also led to an improvement in data protection practices, encouraging organizations to adopt stricter security measures and promote a culture of respect for privacy.

- Strengthening Trust: Compliance with stringent regulations strengthens public trust in AI systems by promoting wider and safer adoption of these technologies.

# 9 From collection to deactivation: strategies for managing AI data.

Effective data lifecycle management is a critical component to the success of any artificial intelligence (AI) system. The data lifecycle involves a series of steps, from initial collection to eventual deactivation or deletion of the data.

Each phase of the data lifecycle presents unique challenges and opportunities, and how these phases are managed can significantly impact the efficiency, security, and value of AI systems.

## 9.1 The Importance of the Data Lifecycle in AI

The data lifecycle in AI encompasses all the stages that data goes through, from its creation or collection to its eventual deletion. Each phase of the lifecycle plays a vital role in maintaining the integrity, security, and usefulness of data.

Efficient data lifecycle management ensures that information is always available, secure, and compliant with applicable regulations, while contributing to value creation through accurate analysis and data-driven decision-making.

- Maximizing Value: Proper data lifecycle management allows organizations to extract the most value from data, using it effectively to train AI models and generate meaningful insights.

- Minimizing Risks: Effective management also helps to minimize risks such as security breaches, data loss, and non-compliance with regulations, ensuring that data is handled responsibly throughout its lifecycle.

## 9.2    Phases of the data lifecycle in AI.

The data lifecycle can be divided into several distinct phases, each with its own challenges and best practices. Below, we explore each of these phases in detail.

### 9.2.1    Data Collection.

Data collection is the first phase of the lifecycle and involves capturing information from various sources, such as sensors, IoT devices, databases, social networks, and user interactions. Effective data collection is crucial to ensure that AI models are trained with relevant, accurate, and comprehensive information.

- Data sources: Data can be collected from a wide range of sources, including IoT devices, enterprise systems, social networks, external APIs, and more.

  The diversity of data sources increases the complexity of collection, but it also provides opportunities for richer, more detailed insights.

- Quality and relevance: The quality of the data collected is critical. Inaccurate or irrelevant data can compromise the effectiveness of AI models.

  It is important to implement quality controls during the collection phase to ensure that only valuable and accurate data is captured.

- Compliance and consent: Data collection must be carried out in compliance with privacy regulations, such as the GDPR and LGPD.

  This includes obtaining consent from individuals for the collection of their data and ensuring that data is collected in an ethical and transparent manner.

### 9.2.2   Data Storage.

After collection, the data needs to be stored in a secure and organized way so that it can be easily accessed and used. The storage phase involves important decisions about storage infrastructure, data security, and governance.

- Choice of infrastructure: Data can be stored in data warehouses, data lakes, or cloud storage systems. The choice of infrastructure depends on the volume of data, the need for fast access, and security considerations.

- Security and encryption: Protecting stored data is essential. Encryption techniques, both in transit and at rest, must be applied to protect data from unauthorized access and security breaches.

- Data governance: Establishing governance policies is important to ensure that data is managed consistently and in accordance with organizational guidelines.

     This includes defining who has access to the data, how it can be used, and how the quality of the data will be maintained over time.

### 9.2.3   Data Processing.

Data processing involves preparing the data for analysis, including cleaning, transforming, and integrating different data sets. This phase is crucial to ensure that the data is in a format that can be used by AI models.

- Data cleansing: Data cleansing is a critical step that removes duplicates, corrects errors, and fills gaps in the data. The quality of processing directly impacts the effectiveness of AI models.

- Data transformation: Raw data often needs to be transformed into a format that can be used by AI algorithms. This can include normalizing, aggregating, and reducing the dimensionality of data.

- Data integration: In many cases, data needs to be integrated from multiple sources. Effective integration ensures that data is combined cohesively, allowing for comprehensive and accurate analysis.

9.2.4   Data analysis.

Data analysis is the phase in which processed data is used to train AI models, generate insights, and make decisions. This phase includes applying machine learning algorithms and other analytical techniques to extract value from the data.

- Model training: During training, data is used to teach AI models to recognize patterns and make predictions. The quality of the input data is critical to the performance of the model.

  - Validation and testing: After training, models need to be validated and tested to ensure that they generalize well to new data. This step involves using validation datasets that were not used during training.

  - Generating insights: In addition to training AI models, data analytics can also be used to identify trends, patterns, and anomalies in the data, providing valuable insights for decision-making.

9.2.5   Data archiving.

Not all data needs to be kept accessible indefinitely. The archiving phase involves moving data that is no longer actively used to long-term storage, where it can be retrieved if needed.

- Archiving decision: Determining what data should be archived and what should be kept accessible is a strategic decision. Historical data that is no longer needed for daily operations can be archived to free up resources.

- Archiving methods: Archived data should be stored in a way that ensures its long-term integrity and security. Techniques such as compression and encryption are often used to protect archived data.

- Compliance and retention: Data retention policies must comply with applicable regulations, ensuring that data is kept for as long as necessary and deleted when it is no longer required.

### 9.2.6 Data Deletion and Deactivation.

Data deletion or deactivation is the final phase of the data lifecycle. This phase involves securely removing the data that is no longer needed, ensuring that it cannot be accessed or recovered.

- Deletion policies: Establishing clear policies for data deletion is essential to ensure that information is removed securely and in compliance with regulations. This includes the physical destruction of storage media and the overwriting of data on hard drives.

- Minimizing risk: Secure data deletion minimizes the risks of security and compliance breaches. Certified data deletion tools can be utilized to ensure that data is unrecoverable after deletion.

### 9.3 Challenges in managing the data lifecycle in AI.

Data lifecycle management in AI presents several challenges, which can impact the effectiveness and safety of AI systems.

1. Complexity and scalability.

   Managing the lifecycle of large volumes of data, especially in AI environments, can be complex and challenging.

   As the volume of data grows, the demands for storage, processing, and analytics also increase, requiring scalable solutions.

   - Infrastructure scalability: Data infrastructures need to be scalable to handle exponential data growth. Cloud storage and distributed processing solutions are often used to meet these demands.

2. Regulatory compliance.

   Compliance with regulations such as GDPR and LGPD is a constant challenge. Organizations need to ensure that their data management practices are aligned with legal requirements, which can be particularly challenging in international contexts.

   - Monitoring and compliance: Organizations should implement continuous monitoring systems to ensure that data is managed in accordance with regulations, avoiding penalties and maintaining user trust.

3. Data security.

   Data security is a critical concern at every stage of the lifecycle. Cyber threats are constantly evolving, and organizations must always be one step ahead to protect their data.

   - Threat protection: Implementing robust security measures, such as encryption, access control, and activity monitoring, is essential to protect data from unauthorized access and other threats.

9.4    Best practices for data lifecycle management in AI.

Ensuring efficient data lifecycle management in AI requires the adoption of best practices that optimize each phase of the cycle.

1. Lifecycle Automation.

   Automating parts of the data lifecycle can improve efficiency and reduce human error. Automated data management tools can be used for tasks such as data collection, processing, and deletion.

   Automated Tools: Solutions such as automated ETL (Extract, Transform, Load) and intelligent archiving systems can help manage large volumes of data with greater efficiency.

2. Data governance.

   Implementing strong data governance is essential to ensure that data is managed consistently and in accordance with organizational policies.

   • Governance policies: Establishing clear policies for data management, including definitions of accountability, access control, and data quality, is critical to the success of data governance.

3. Education and training.

   Training teams to follow data management best practices is crucial. This includes training on regulatory compliance, data security, and the importance of efficient data lifecycle management.

- Continuous training: Promote continuous training of employees to ensure that they are up-to-date on best practices and the latest regulations in data management.

# 10 Conclusion.

We have reached the end of a deep and challenging journey, where we explore the essence of Information Architecture and its central role in the era of Artificial Intelligence.

Throughout this book, we've seen how data, when properly organized and structured, can be transformed into valuable information, and how that information is the foundation for generating knowledge that powers the intelligent systems that are shaping our world.

Information architecture is not just a technical science. It is the link that connects raw data to applicable knowledge, a practice that permeates all levels of Artificial Intelligence – from model training to analysis and interpretation of results. In this sense, its relevance is increasingly crucial for the development of innovative solutions that directly impact businesses, governments, and society.

We have seen how structured data is critical to the effectiveness of AI models and how semantic modeling allows machines to understand the context behind the information.

We also explored fake news checking, a clear example of how AI can be used to improve the quality of information in our society, combating disinformation that threatens our democratic coexistence.

We understand that digital transformation is not limited to technology; it requires a strategic vision that includes ethics, data governance, privacy protection, and responsibility in the use of AI.

The ethical challenges discussed throughout the chapters show that the role of Artificial Intelligence and Information Architecture professionals goes beyond developing efficient systems; It is also about ensuring that technology is used for the good of society.

By addressing data integration and the challenges of standardization, it became clear that interoperability between AI systems and the ability to handle massive volumes of data are essential for the continued advancement of intelligent technologies.

And as we face these challenges, new opportunities emerge, especially with the development of more flexible data structures and the rise of deep learning technologies.

Information Architecture, as we have seen, is the invisible foundation on which artificial intelligence stands. Without a solid data structure, without understanding context, and without careful information management, even the most advanced models will fail. This book was an invitation for you, the reader, to build this foundation, not only as a technical professional, but as an agent of transformation.

We are in a historic moment of great changes. Artificial Intelligence and Information Architecture offer a vast field of possibilities, but it is up to each of us to ensure that these technologies are used responsibly and wisely.

The transformation that is coming will depend not only on technical innovations, but on an ethical and strategic vision of how information will be managed and applied.

This volume is part of a larger collection, "Artificial Intelligence: The Power of Data," with 49 volumes that explore, in depth, different aspects of AI and data science.

The other volumes address equally crucial topics, such as the integration of AI systems, predictive analytics, and the use of advanced algorithms for decision-making.

By purchasing and reading the other books in the collection, you will have a holistic and deep view that will allow you not only to optimize data governance, but also to enhance the impact of artificial intelligence on your operations.

In a data-driven world, your ability to make sense of this avalanche of information will not only be your competitive advantage, but also your contribution to building a smarter, more ethical, and more innovative future.

# 11 Glossary.

1. Access and security. The metadata must contain sufficient information to determine data access profiles. It must be possible to identify which users can read, update, delete, or enter data into the database. There should also be information about who manages these access profiles and how to contact the Database Administrator.

2. Remote Access. It is the ability to access information or systems from a remote location, using networks or technologies such as VPN (Virtual Private Network).

3. Restricted Access. Restriction of access to data only to authorized persons, ensuring the security and privacy of information.

4. Data Analysis. It is the process of examining, cleaning, transforming, and modeling data in order to uncover useful information, trends, and patterns. Data analytics helps you make informed decisions and extract valuable insights.

5. Text Analysis. It is the process of extracting meaningful information from a text, such as themes, feelings, entities mentioned, or trends, through computational techniques.

6. Analytics: The process of analyzing and interpreting data to identify key patterns, trends, and insights that can be used to make informed decisions and improve business performance.

7. Anonymization. Make data anonymous and cannot be associated with a person. This practice is usual when it comes to confidential data.

8. Anonymization. Personally identifiable data removal process to ensure privacy and regulatory compliance.

9. Machine Learning. It is an area of artificial intelligence that involves the development of algorithms capable of learning and improving based on data. Machine learning models are trained to make predictions or classifications based on past examples.

10. Thematic area. It is the division of the company into business areas, which define the management of the Encyclopedia's data objects.

11. Storage. Proper maintenance of data in a secure and reliable system to ensure its preservation.

12. Information architect. Professional systems analyst who acts as a modeler of the information that will be present at the data mart.

13. Information Architecture. It is the design and structural organization of information systems, such as websites and applications, in order to facilitate navigation and understanding of information by users.

14. Data Update. The history of updates is usually maintained by the database itself, but defining a metadata element, indicating the dates of data update, can help the user when checking the freshness of the data and the consistency of the data warehouse's time dimension.

15. Database: An organized set of related information, usually stored electronically. A database is designed to allow for the efficient retrieval, updating, and analysis of this information.

16. Bibliometrics. It is the use of quantitative methods to analyze scientific production, such as citation counts, impact indexes, and co-authorship analysis. It helps to assess the visibility and influence of the search.

17. Big Data: A term used to describe a large volume of complex data that is difficult to process and analyze using traditional methods. Big Data involves collecting, storing, analyzing, and interpreting this data to gain insights and make informed decisions.

18. Brainstorm. A way of conducting group work to generate ideas, with the same objective and coordination, which is characterized by the oral formulation of the same without concern for logic or self-censorship.

19. Brainwriting. A way of conducting group work for the generation of ideas, with the same objective and coordination, which is characterized by the written formulation of the same without concern for logic or self-censorship.

20. Business Intelligence. A set of theories, methodologies, processes, technologies and structures that transform large amounts of data that, alone, do not mean much, into essential information for good management.

21. Access Path. (or logical access) is the means by which one reads, deletes, or alters a tuple from an attribute relationship.

22. Test case. Set of conditions used to test a use case.

23. Use case. A modeling technique used to describe what a new data mart should do. It is built based on the functional requirements of the project. It typically refers to a project interface.

24. Cataloguing. Organization of data in a catalog or directory, allowing for quick identification and retrieval of information.

25. Information catalog. Information provided by the data models. They must contain sufficient information to extract the knowledge stored in the Organization's databases. Description of the information, logical storage location (owner, table, geographic object, data mart...), physical storage location, responsible for updating the data that make up the information, validity and correlation with other information.

26. Checklist. It is a control instrument, composed of a set of conducts, names, items or tasks that must be remembered and/or followed. A checklist.

27. Cybersecurity. It is the protection of information and computer systems against cyber-attacks, such as malware, hackers, and data theft.

28. Data Lifecycle. A process that encompasses everything from data collection to disposal, considering its usefulness and relevance over time.

29. Information Science. It is a discipline that studies the processes of creation, organization, retrieval, and use of information, with the aim of improving the way information is organized and accessed.

30. Cover. Geographic or temporal coverage of a data.

31. Collection. The process of gathering data from different sources, whether structured or unstructured.

32. Sharing. Facilitating controlled access to data between different users and systems, ensuring collaboration and information exchange.

33. Quality control. Measurement of how well an item conforms to its specifications.

34. Schedule. Planning and control instrument in which the activities and tasks to be performed during an estimated period of time are defined and detailed.

35. Digital Curation. It is the process of selecting, organizing, and preserving valuable digital content to ensure its accessibility and usability in the long term.

36. Public data. Any data generated or under government custody that does not have its access restricted by specific legislation.

37. Personal data. Private data of each person.

38. Sensitive data. These are data temporarily subject to the restriction of public access due to their indispensability for the security of society and the State".

39. Data Archiving. It's the process of moving old or little-used data to a long-term storage location, freeing up space on more active systems and maintaining regulatory compliance.

40. Data Cleansing. It is the process of identifying and correcting errors, inconsistencies, and duplicate data in databases, ensuring the quality and reliability of the information.

41. Data Dictionary. It is a document or system that contains a detailed description of the data, including its meaning, format, origin, relationships, and associated business rules.

42. Data Governance Council. It is a committee responsible for establishing policies, guidelines, and standards related to data governance in an organization, ensuring its compliance and quality.

43. Data Governance Framework. It is a framework that establishes the components, principles, processes, and metrics to implement effective and sustainable data governance in an organization.

44. Data Governance. It is the set of policies, processes, and procedures to manage, protect, and ensure the quality of an organization's data, ensuring its compliance with laws and regulations.

45. Data Migration. It is the process of transferring data from an old system to a new one, usually involving steps of cleaning, converting, and validating the data.

46. Data Mining. It is the practice of exploring large data sets in search of patterns, trends, and useful information that can be used for strategic decision-making.

47. Data Ownership. It refers to assigning responsibility and ownership of data to individuals or departments within an organization, ensuring its proper management and protection.

48. Data Privacy. It refers to the practices and regulations for protecting the privacy of personal data, ensuring that information is collected, stored, and used in a secure and consenting manner.

49. Data Profiling. It is the exploratory analysis of data, identifying its format, structure, distribution, and quality, in order to understand its relevance and suitability for certain analyses and decisions.

50. Data Profiling. It is the exploratory analysis of data, identifying its format, structure, distribution, and quality, in order to understand its relevance and suitability for certain analyses and decisions.

51. Data Stewardship. It is the process of designating individuals responsible for the management, control, and governance of data in an organization, ensuring its quality, integrity, and compliance with policies and regulations.

52. Data Strategy. It is a strategic plan that defines the objectives, guidelines, and priorities related to the management and use of data in an organization, aligning with the strategic vision and objectives.

53. Data Visualization. It is the graphical representation of data, through graphs, tables, and other visual elements, to facilitate the understanding and identification of patterns and trends.

54. Data warehouse. It is a centralized repository that stores large amounts of data from different sources, allowing for advanced queries and analytics to aid in decision-making.

55. Data warehouse. A Data Warehouse is a computer system used to store information related to an organization's activities in databases, in a consolidated way.

56. Dataset. Dataset. It is the file generated from the original database. It needs to follow open data norms and standards for its publication to be accepted on the Portal.

57. Business definitions. These definitions are the most important information contained in the metadata. Each data element must be supported by a definition of it in the context of the Business Area. The method of maintaining this information must also be very consistent, so that the user can easily obtain definitions for the desired information. In these definitions, references to other metadata that require a second search for better understanding should be avoided.

58. Applicant. Person who requests part or all of a Data Warehouse project.

59. Data dictionary. Collection that describes and defines the meaning of all the data that make up the information universe of a system and allows the verification of consistency between the various models.

60. Dictionaryization. The detailed record of the persistent elements that make up a predefined universe.

61. Copyright. These are laws that protect the rights of creators of intellectual works, such as texts, images, music, and software. They regulate the use, reproduction and distribution of these works.

62. Information Ecology. It is the study of the complex interactions between information, systems, and users in a specific environment. It analyzes how the environment affects the creation, use, and dissemination of information.

63. Software Engineering. It is the process of developing, testing, and maintaining software. It involves applying engineering principles to create reliable, efficient, and secure software systems.

64. Enrichment. Adding additional information to existing data to improve its quality and context.

65. Information Ethics. It refers to the moral principles and responsibilities related to the use, access, disclosure, and handling of information. It involves issues such as privacy, security, and equitable access to information.

66. ETL (Extract, Transform, Load). It is the process of extracting data from various sources, transforming it according to business rules, and loading it into a destination location, such as a data warehouse.

67. OLAP tool. Online Analytical Processing. It is a tool that provides its user with the ability to manipulate and analyze a large volume of data from multiple perspectives.

68. Information Flow. It is the continuous movement of information between different sources, users, and systems. It involves processes of creation, transmission, storage and use of information. It refers to any medium or resource that provides information, such as books, articles, websites, databases, among others.

69. Data sources. These are the data that usually come from transactional systems and must be extracted and loaded into the Data Transport Area (Intermediate or Stage Area). Data sources that are structured in other ways and data from sources outside the company may also be considered.

70. Data format. Every data element should have identified its size and type of data.

71. Information Management: The process of collecting, organizing, storing, retrieving, and disseminating information efficiently and effectively, ensuring its integrity, security, and accessibility.

72. Project management. Application of knowledge, skills, tools, and techniques to project activities in order to meet your requirements.

73. Knowledge Management. It is the process of identifying, capturing, storing, and sharing knowledge within an organization, aiming to improve performance and promote innovation.

74. Project Time Management. It includes the processes required to achieve project completion on time.

75. Project Risk Management. It includes the processes related to risk management planning, risk identification and analysis, risk responses, and risk monitoring and control of a project.

76. Data manager. Professional of the publishing institution responsible for establishing the guidelines of the opening process in the institution.

77. Data Governance. Set of policies, procedures, and practices to ensure data quality, reliability, and compliance.

78. Data Governance. It is the set of processes, policies, and guidelines to ensure the proper and effective management of data in an organization. It involves defining responsibilities, quality policies, compliance, and data security.

79. Governance. The governance of the affairs of any institution, including non-governmental institutions.

80. Historic. Record changes to an artifact, table, project, data mart, or data warehouse.

81. Homologation. Proof, by the client and other interested parties, that the product resulting from the software project meets the acceptance criteria previously established with it. It includes elements of verification and validation of the product, all or parts of the product, selected in agreement with the customer, and its main goal is to obtain product acceptance.

82. Data Hosting. Technology structure responsible for storing data. A database performs this function.

83. Identification. Concatenation of words and short forms, natural or derived, that fulfill the function of distinguishing, generically or specifically, the object of data and transmitting its meaning.

84. Indexing. It is the process of assigning indexing terms or keywords to documents to facilitate their identification and retrieval. It is an important step in the organization and search for information.

85. Data quality indicators. Quality indices can be created based on the origin of the data, number of processing done on this data, atomic values X summarized values, level of use of the data, etc.

86. Information: Data that has been processed, organized, and interpreted in a meaningful way, resulting in knowledge or understanding.

87. IT infrastructure. It refers to the set of equipment, systems, and networks required to support information technology operations in an organization, such as servers, storage devices, and network cables.

88. Integration. Combining different data sets to create a unified and complete view.

89. Integrity. It refers to the quality of the data, ensuring that it is free from errors, inconsistencies, and duplicates.

90. Artificial Intelligence: It is an area of computer science that focuses on creating systems or machines capable of performing tasks that usually require human intelligence. It involves skills such as learning, reasoning, pattern recognition, and decision-making.

91. Artificial Intelligence: A field of computer science that develops systems and programs capable of performing tasks that often require human intelligence, such as pattern recognition, decision-making, and learning.

92. Human-Computer Interaction. It is the field of study that focuses on the design and development of computational systems that are easy to use and interact effectively with people. It involves understanding the needs and behaviors of users to create intuitive and efficient interfaces.

93. Cleaning. Data treatment stage, removing redundant, inconsistent or incomplete information.

94. Computational linguistics. It is the study and development of algorithms and systems to automate natural language processing, including tasks such as speech recognition, machine translation, and sentiment analysis.

95. Information Literacy. It is the ability to locate, evaluate, use, and communicate information effectively. It promotes research skills, critical thinking, and informed decision-making.

96. Machine Learning. It is an AI technique that allows systems to learn from data without being explicitly programmed. Machine learning models are trained to recognize patterns and make decisions based on those patterns.

97. Master Data. It is the fundamental and central data of an organization, such as customers, products, suppliers, which are shared and used in different systems and processes.

98. Traceability matrix. Diagram that contrasts elements that map each other.

99. Metadata. Data, especially digital data, takes many forms. Voice chats, text messages or social networks communicate data. Digital, banking, or commercial transactions involve the transfer of data. Web content, digitized and transferred entertainment, databases, and information repositories of all kinds are examples of data publications. The metadata describes what this data is. They provide information about this data. This is quite simple. However, if we analyze this in detail, we find that "describing" the data is a rigorous technical exercise and a problem fraught with sociopolitical implications.

100. Metadata. Descriptive information about the data, such as its origin, format, content, and meaning.

101. Metadata. It is additional information that describes the data, such as its meaning, origin, format, and relationships, facilitating the understanding and proper use of the information.

102. Metadata. It is descriptive information that describes the attributes and characteristics of an information resource, such as title, author, creation date, format, among others.

103. Methodology. Structured set of practices that can be repeatable during the software production process.

104. Data Mining. It is the process of finding patterns, relationships, and useful information in large amounts of data. It involves techniques such as data extraction, transformation, and analysis.

105. Data modeling. It consists of the Analysis and Planning of the data that will make up the Bank.

106. Monitoring. Continuous monitoring of data to identify changes, trends, and important events.

107. Negotiation. It involves debating with others in order to reach an agreement with them or to reach an agreement.

108. Normalization. Process of organizing data into standardized structures, eliminating redundancies and inconsistencies, aiming to improve the efficiency and integrity of databases.

109. Normalization. Process of transforming the data into a standard format to facilitate comparison and analysis.

110. Ontology. It is a conceptual model that represents the structure of knowledge in a given area. An ontology describes the classes, properties, and relationships between concepts within a specific domain.

111. Organization of Information. It refers to the process of classifying, categorizing, and structuring information to facilitate its retrieval and efficient use.

112. Organization. Systematic organization of data in a logical and accessible way to facilitate future consultation and analysis.

113. Organization chart. A chart that represents the formal structure of an organization. In other words, it is the classic graphical representation of an organizational structure.

114. Origin of the data. Every data element needs to have identified, its origin or the process that generates it. This identification is very important in case you need to know information about the source of the data. This information must be unique, that is, each data must have one and only one source of origin.

115. Standardization. Establishment of rules and conventions to standardize the structure and format of data.

116. Planning. A phase of a project's life cycle composed of processes for successfully planning and managing a project; To this end, they develop the Management Plan, which mainly includes the scope of the project, its costs, the activities to be developed, the human and material resources required, the necessary communications, the risks to be faced, the quality to be guaranteed, and the needs for acquisitions and purchases.

117. Action Plan. Document that describes what will be done, in what timeframe, by whom.

118. Project plan. Document that formalizes all the planning to execute, control and close the project. Through it, it is possible to know the objective of the project, what are the estimated costs and time, what resources will be involved for its execution, and much more.

119. Plan. Document that outlines how a goal will be achieved and what will be needed to achieve it.

120. PMI. Project Management Institute. It is a non-profit organization that aims to disseminate best practices in project management around the world.

121. Premise. Factors associated with the scope of the project that, for planning purposes, are assumed to be true, real, or certain, without the need for proof or demonstration.

122. Information Preservation. It involves actions to ensure the longevity and accessibility of information over time, protecting it from technological loss, deterioration, or obsolescence.

123. Provision of service. One of the three pillars that sustain Open Government. It improves the effectiveness of the State by encouraging cooperation between society, the different levels of government, and private initiative.

124. Data Privacy: The right and measures taken to protect the personal information of individuals by ensuring that such data is collected and used in accordance with applicable laws and regulations, with respect to the privacy and security of personal data. This includes informed consent practices, anonymization, encryption, and access control to personal data.

125. Procedure. Step-by-step description of a sequence of tasks for carrying out an activity. Describes tasks to be performed and identifies rules for developing them.

126. Iterative process. In a software lifecycle context, it is the type of process that involves managing a chain of executable releases.

127. Process. It is a set of interrelated actions and activities carried out to achieve a previously defined set of products, results or services.

128. Product. A produced item that is quantifiable and that can be a finished element or a component.

129. Project. Temporal effort undertaken to create a unique product, service, or result.

130. Data Quality. It represents the level of accuracy, completeness, consistency, and timeliness of the data, ensuring its reliability and usefulness in decision-making.

131. Qualification. A semantic component of a name that, when applied to identifications, sentences, or classes of attributes, refines the meaning provided by the data object to which it applies, through successive specification of properties, until the data object can be distinguished univocally by the name thus composed.

132. Traceability. Complete and detailed record of the history and transformations undergone by data over time.

133. Information Retrieval. It is the process of finding and providing relevant information from a collection of data. It includes indexing, searching, and retrieving information techniques.

134. Resources. Specialized human resources, teams, services, supplies, raw materials, materials, budgets, or resources needed to carry out the schedule activities.

135. Social Networks. They are online platforms that allow individuals to connect, share information, and interact virtually. Examples include Facebook, Twitter, and linkedin.

136. Reference. Harnessing the name of another data object for use as identification.

137. Transformation rules. They are considered to be the codified Business Rules. These rules are generated at the time of extraction, cleaning and grouping of data from the Operating Systems. Each hard-coded transformation rule must be associated with a Metadata element. If more than one application contains the same transformation rule, it should be ensured that they are identical.

138. Institutional Repository. It is a system used to store, preserve, and make available the intellectual production of an institution, such as scientific articles, theses, dissertations, and reports.

139. Problem solving. It entails both defining the problem (causes and symptoms) and making decisions (analyzing the problem to identify viable solutions and make a decision).

140. Restriction. Limitations imposed on the project.

141. Result. Outputs or documents generated from an information source.

142. Road Map. Planning tool that has the function of mapping the path to be taken to obtain the expected result in a project.

143.    Information Security. It encompasses measures and protocols to protect data from unauthorized access, loss, tampering, and privacy violations.

144.    Information Security: Measures and practices adopted to protect information against unauthorized access, misuse, disclosure, modification or destruction, ensuring its confidentiality, integrity and availability.

145.    Corporate information systems. Information systems that are used by various areas.

146.    Information Systems. A system, automated or manual, that comprises people, machines, and/or organized methods for collecting, processing, transmitting, and disseminating data that represents information to the user. Oracle is a database system that emerged in the late 1970s, when Larry Ellison saw an opportunity that other companies had not realized when he found the description of a working prototype of a relational database and discovered that no company had committed to commercializing this technology.

147.    Information Systems: Sets of interrelated elements that collect, process, store, and distribute information to support decision-making and the functioning of organizations.

148.    Taxonomy. It is a classification system used to organize information into hierarchical categories. It helps in navigating and finding relevant information.

149.    User. People who use the technology element.

150.    Validation. Verification of data quality and integrity, ensuring its accuracy and consistency.

151. Data Visualization. It is the graphical representation of information to facilitate understanding and analysis. Charts, maps, diagrams, and infographics are examples of data visualization techniques.

152. Visualization. Graphical representation of data in an intuitive way, facilitating understanding and analysis by users.

153. Semantic web. It is an extension of the World Wide Web that aims to make information understandable to both humans and machines. It uses ontologies and metadata to assign meaning to data and enable better organization and retrieval of information on the Web.

# 12 FAQ.

1. Question: What is information?

Information is a set of organized and meaningful data, which has value and can be used for decision-making or to obtain knowledge on a given subject.

2. Question: What is the relationship between information and science?

Information is fundamental for the development of science, as it is through it that the data collected, the results of research, and scientific discoveries are recorded.

Science uses information as a basis for producing and sharing knowledge.

3. Question: What is technology?

Technology is the set of knowledge and techniques applied in practice to produce, develop or improve products, processes and services. It involves the use of tools, machines, equipment, and systems to solve problems and satisfy human needs.

4. Question: What is the relationship between information and technology?

Information is essential for the functioning of technology. It is processed, stored, and transmitted through technological systems, such as computers, communication networks, and electronic devices.

Technology uses information as raw material to create and deliver innovative services, products, and solutions.

5. Question: How do science, information, and technology complement each other?

Science produces knowledge through the analysis of information. Technology uses this knowledge to develop innovative solutions.

Information is the element that connects science to technology, providing the data necessary for scientific advancement and technological development.

6. Question: In what aspects is information important for society?

Information is important to society in several aspects, such as enabling access to knowledge, making informed decisions, promoting transparency, facilitating communication and the exchange of ideas, driving innovation and economic development, as well as being fundamental for education and social progress.

7. How does science contribute to the advancement of society?

Science contributes to the advancement of society by providing knowledge and solutions to complex problems.

It enables the development of new technologies, advances in medicine, understanding of natural and social phenomena, as well as promoting innovation, sustainability, and economic progress.

8. What are the main impacts of technology on everyday life?

Technology has significant impacts on daily life, such as facilitating communication and connection between people, streamlining tasks and processes, allowing access to information and services, providing entertainment and leisure, improving quality of life, boosting productivity, and creating new business opportunities.

9. How can science, information and technology be allies in solving problems?

Science provides knowledge and methods for understanding and solving complex problems. Information is the basis for the generation of scientific and technological knowledge.

Technology, in turn, uses this knowledge to develop practical and innovative solutions. Together, these three areas can collaborate to solve challenges in the most diverse areas, such as health, environment, security, among others.

10. What are the ethical responsibilities associated with information management?

The ethical responsibilities associated with information management include ensuring data privacy and security, respecting copyright and intellectual property, avoiding discriminatory and unfair practices in the use of information, ensuring transparency in the collection and use of data, and acting in accordance with the principles of honesty, integrity, and impartiality.

11. How can science, information and technology contribute to environmental sustainability?

Science can provide insights into the environmental impacts of human activities and help identify solutions to reduce those impacts. Information is critical for monitoring and evaluating natural resources, as well as for sustainable decision-making.

Technology, in turn, can be used for the development of clean technologies, renewable energies and more efficient environmental management systems.

12. What are the challenges of information management in the digital age?

Some challenges of information management in the digital age include the enormous amount of data available, the need to ensure the security and privacy of personal data, the rapid technological evolution that demands constant updating of systems and practices, the difficulty of filtering and finding relevant information in the midst of excess data and ensuring the reliability and quality of the data collected.

13. How can science, information and technology promote digital inclusion?

Science can provide knowledge and research to understand digital inequalities and propose solutions to overcome them. The information can be used to raise awareness about the importance of access to technology and the development of digital skills.

Technology, in turn, can offer accessible and inclusive solutions, such as adapted devices and software, as well as training and digital inclusion programs.

14. What are the impacts of the spread of false information on society?

The spread of false information, also known as fake news, can cause significant damage to society. These include the spread of misinformation, the manipulation of public opinions, the spread of conspiracy theories, social division, distrust in institutions and the media, as well as potentially affecting informed decision-making.

Combating the spread of false information is essential to preserve the integrity of the democratic process and promote a fairer and more informed society.

15. How can science, information and technology contribute to education?

Science, through research and studies, expands human knowledge and provides solid foundations for education. Information, whether in books, scientific articles, or online resources, is essential for learning and skill development.

Technology, such as educational platforms, digital resources, and interactive tools, can expand access to education, make it more personalized, and facilitate the teaching-learning process.

16. How does science contribute to the advancement of society?

Science contributes to the advancement of society by providing knowledge and solutions to complex problems. It enables the development of new technologies, advances in medicine, understanding of natural and social phenomena, as well as promoting innovation, sustainability, and economic progress.

17. What are the main impacts of technology on everyday life?

Technology has significant impacts on daily life, such as facilitating communication and connection between people, streamlining tasks and processes, allowing access to information and services, providing entertainment and leisure, improving quality of life, boosting productivity, and creating new business opportunities.

18. How can science, information and technology be allies in solving problems?

Science provides knowledge and methods for understanding and solving complex problems. Information is the basis for the generation of scientific and technological knowledge.

Technology, in turn, uses this knowledge to develop practical and innovative solutions. Together, these three areas can collaborate to solve challenges in the most diverse areas, such as health, environment, security, among others.

19. What are the ethical responsibilities associated with information management?

The ethical responsibilities associated with information management include ensuring data privacy and security, respecting copyright and intellectual property, avoiding discriminatory and unfair practices in the use of information, ensuring transparency in the collection and use of data, and acting in accordance with the principles of honesty, integrity, and impartiality.

20. What are the challenges of information management in the digital age?

Some challenges of information management in the digital age include the enormous amount of data available, the need to ensure the security and privacy of personal data, the rapid technological evolution that demands constant updating of systems and practices, the difficulty of filtering and finding relevant information in the midst of excess data and ensuring the reliability and quality of the data collected.

21. How can information, science and technology be applied in the health sector?

The information can be used to share medical knowledge, research, and effective practices. Science contributes to the advancement of medical treatments, accurate diagnoses, and disease prevention.

The technology is applied in advanced medical equipment, electronic health records, telemedicine, and drug development.

22. What are the ethical challenges related to the collection and use of personal information?

Ethical challenges include ensuring informed consent, privacy and security of personal information, preventing data misuse and discrimination, and ensuring transparency and accountability in the handling of information.

# 13 References.

ALLCOTT, H.; GENTZKOW, M. (2017). "Social Media and Fake News in the 2016 Election." Journal of Economic Perspectives, 31(2), 211-236.

BATINI, C.; SCANNAPIECO, M. (2006). Data Quality: Concepts, Methodologies and Techniques. Springer.

BERNERS-LEE, T.; HENDLER, J.; LASSILA, O. (2001). "The Semantic Web." Scientific American, 284(5), 28-37.

BUOLAMWINI, J.; GEBRU, T. (2018). "Gender Shades: Intersectional Accuracy Disparities in Commercial Gender Classification." Proceedings of Machine Learning Research, 81, 1-15.

CHEN, P. P. (1976). "The Entity-Relationship Model: Toward a Unified View of Data." ACM Transactions on Database Systems (TODS), 1(1), 9-36.

CODD, E. F. (1970). "A Relational Model of Data for Large Shared Data Banks." Communications of the ACM, 13(6), 377-387.

DEVLIN, J.; CHANG, M. W.; LEE, K.; TOUTANOVA, K. (2018). "BERT: Pre-training of Deep Bidirectional Transformers for Language Understanding." arXiv preprint arXiv:1810.04805.

DOMINGOS, P. (2015). The Master Algorithm: How the Quest for the Ultimate Learning Machine Will Remake Our World. Basic Books.

GOODFELLOW, I.; BENGIO, Y.; COURVILLE, A. (2016). Deep Learning. MIT Press.

GRUBER, T. R. (1995). "Toward Principles for the Design of Ontologies Used for Knowledge Sharing." International Journal of Human-Computer Studies, 43(5-6), 907-928.

HINTON, G.; LE CUN, Y.; BENGIO, Y. (2015). "Deep Learning." Nature, 521(7553), 436-444.

INMON, W. H. (1992). Building the Data Warehouse. Wiley.

INMON, W. H.; LINDSTEDT, D.; LEADBETTER, M. (2010). Data Architecture: A Primer for the Data Scientist. Morgan Kaufmann.

KANTARDZIC, M. (2011). Data Mining: Concepts, Models, Methods, and Algorithms. Wiley-IEEE Press.

MACHADO, R. P.; BARCELLOS, C. H. (2020). LGPD Comments on the General Law for the Protection of Personal Data. Editora Revista dos Tribunais.

MARZ, N.; WARREN, J. (2015). Big Data: Principles and Best Practices of Scalable Real-time Data Systems. Manning Publications.

MIKOLOV, T.; CHEN, K.; CORRADO, G.; DEAN, J. (2013). "Efficient Estimation of Word Representations in Vector Space." arXiv preprint arXiv:1301.3781.

NEO4J, Inc. (2020). Graph Databases: New Opportunities for Connected Data. O'Reilly Media.

OLSON, J. E. (2003). Data Quality: The Accuracy Dimension. Morgan Kaufmann.

O'NEILL, C. (2016). Weapons of Math Destruction: How Big Data Increases Inequality and Threatens Democracy. Crown Publishing Group.

PYLE, D. (1999). Data Preparation for Data Mining. Morgan Kaufmann.

REDMAN, T. C. (2001). Data Quality: The Field Guide. Digital Press.

REED, C.; NGUYEN, J. (2019). Data Protection and Privacy: The Age of Intelligent Machines. Oxford University Press.

SHANNON, C. E. (1948). "A Mathematical Theory of Communication." Bell System Technical Journal, 27(3), 379-423.

TURING, A. M. (1950). "Computing Machinery and Intelligence." Mind, 59(236), 433-460.

VOIGHT, P.; VON DEM BUSSCHE, A. (2017). The EU General Data Protection Regulation (GDPR): A Practical Guide. Springer International Publishing.

VON NEUMANN, J. (1958). The Computer and the Brain. Yale University Press.

VOSOUGHI, S.; ROY, D.; ARAL, S. (2018). "The Spread of True and False News Online." Science, 359(6380), 1146-1151.

ZANNETTI, G.; SANTOS, A. P.; MACÊDO, D. F. (2019). "Detecting Fake News on Social Networks Using Machine Learning." IEEE Latin America Transactions, 17(12), 2047-2053.

ZUBOFF, S. (2019). The Age of Surveillance Capitalism: The Fight for a Human Future at the New Frontier of Power. PublicAffairs.

# 14 Discover the Complete Collection "Artificial Intelligence and the Power of Data" – An Invitation to Transform Your Career and Knowledge.

The "Artificial Intelligence and the Power of Data" Collection was created for those who want not only to understand Artificial Intelligence (AI), but also to apply it strategically and practically.

In a series of carefully crafted volumes, I unravel complex concepts in a clear and accessible manner, ensuring the reader has a thorough understanding of AI and its impact on modern societies.

No matter your level of familiarity with the topic, this collection turns the difficult into the didactic, the theoretical into the applicable, and the technical into something powerful for your career.

## 14.1 Why buy this collection?

We are living through an unprecedented technological revolution, where AI is the driving force in areas such as medicine, finance, education, government, and entertainment.

The collection "Artificial Intelligence and the Power of Data" dives deep into all these sectors, with practical examples and reflections that go far beyond traditional concepts.

You'll find both the technical expertise and the ethical and social implications of AI encouraging you to see this technology not just as a tool, but as a true agent of transformation.

Each volume is a fundamental piece of this innovative puzzle: from machine learning to data governance and from ethics to practical application.

With the guidance of an experienced author who combines academic research with years of hands-on practice, this collection is more than a set of books — it's an indispensable guide for anyone looking to navigate and excel in this burgeoning field.

## 14.2    Target Audience of this Collection?

This collection is for everyone who wants to play a prominent role in the age of AI:

- ✓ Tech Professionals: Receive deep technical insights to expand their skills.

- ✓ Students and the Curious: have access to clear explanations that facilitate the understanding of the complex universe of AI.

- ✓ Managers, business leaders, and policymakers will also benefit from the strategic vision on AI, which is essential for making well-informed decisions.

- ✓ Professionals in Career Transition: Professionals in career transition or interested in specializing in AI will find here complete material to build their learning trajectory.

## 14.3    Much More Than Technique — A Complete Transformation.

This collection is not just a series of technical books; It is a tool for intellectual and professional growth.

With it, you go far beyond theory: each volume invites you to a deep reflection on the future of humanity in a world where machines and algorithms are increasingly present.

This is your invitation to master the knowledge that will define the future and become part of the transformation that Artificial Intelligence brings to the world.

Be a leader in your industry, master the skills the market demands, and prepare for the future with the "Artificial Intelligence and the Power of Data" collection.

This is not just a purchase; It is a decisive investment in your learning and professional development journey.

Prof. Marcão - Marcus Vinícius Pinto

M.Sc. in Information Technology.
Specialist in Artificial Intelligence, Data
Governance and Information Architecture.

## 15  The Books of the Collection.

### 15.1  Data, Information and Knowledge in the era of Artificial Intelligence.

This book essentially explores the theoretical and practical foundations of Artificial Intelligence, from data collection to its transformation into intelligence. It focuses primarily on machine learning, AI training, and neural networks.

### 15.2  From Data to Gold: How to Turn Information into Wisdom in the Age of AI.

This book offers a critical analysis on the evolution of Artificial Intelligence, from raw data to the creation of artificial wisdom, integrating neural networks, deep learning, and knowledge modeling.

It presents practical examples in health, finance, and education, and addresses ethical and technical challenges.

### 15.3  Challenges and Limitations of Data in AI.

The book offers an in-depth analysis of the role of data in the development of AI exploring topics such as quality, bias, privacy, security, and scalability with practical case studies in healthcare, finance, and public safety.

### 15.4  Historical Data in Databases for AI: Structures, Preservation, and Purge.

This book investigates how historical data management is essential to the success of AI projects. It addresses the relevance of ISO standards to ensure quality and safety, in addition to analyzing trends and innovations in data processing.

## 15.5 Controlled Vocabulary for Data Dictionary: A Complete Guide.

This comprehensive guide explores the advantages and challenges of implementing controlled vocabularies in the context of AI and information science. With a detailed approach, it covers everything from the naming of data elements to the interactions between semantics and cognition.

## 15.6 Data Curation and Management for the Age of AI.

This book presents advanced strategies for transforming raw data into valuable insights, with a focus on meticulous curation and efficient data management. In addition to technical solutions, it addresses ethical and legal issues, empowering the reader to face the complex challenges of information.

## 15.7 Information Architecture.

The book addresses data management in the digital age, combining theory and practice to create efficient and scalable AI systems, with insights into modeling and ethical and legal challenges.

## 15.8 Fundamentals: The Essentials of Mastering Artificial Intelligence.

An essential work for anyone who wants to master the key concepts of AI, with an accessible approach and practical examples. The book explores innovations such as Machine Learning and Natural Language Processing, as well as ethical and legal challenges, and offers a clear view of the impact of AI on various industries.

## 15.9 LLMS - Large-Scale Language Models.

This essential guide helps you understand the revolution of Large-Scale Language Models (LLMs) in AI.

The book explores the evolution of GPTs and the latest innovations in human-computer interaction, offering practical insights into their impact on industries such as healthcare, education, and finance.

15.10  Machine Learning: Fundamentals and Advances.

This book offers a comprehensive overview of supervised and unsupervised algorithms, deep neural networks, and federated learning. In addition to addressing issues of ethics and explainability of models.

15.11  Inside Synthetic Minds.

This book reveals how these 'synthetic minds' are redefining creativity, work, and human interactions. This work presents a detailed analysis of the challenges and opportunities provided by these technologies, exploring their profound impact on society.

15.12  The Issue of Copyright.

This book invites the reader to explore the future of creativity in a world where human-machine collaboration is a reality, addressing questions about authorship, originality, and intellectual property in the age of generative AIs.

15.13  1121 Questions and Answers: From Basic to Complex – Part 1 to 4.

Organized into four volumes, these questions serve as essential practical guides to mastering key AI concepts.

Part 1 addresses information, data, geoprocessing, the evolution of artificial intelligence, its historical milestones and basic concepts.

Part 2 delves into complex concepts such as machine learning, natural language processing, computer vision, robotics, and decision algorithms.

Part 3 addresses issues such as data privacy, work automation, and the impact of large-scale language models (LLMs).

Part 4 explores the central role of data in the age of artificial intelligence, delving into the fundamentals of AI and its applications in areas such as mental health, government, and anti-corruption.

15.14   The Definitive Glossary of Artificial Intelligence.

This glossary presents more than a thousand artificial intelligence concepts clearly explained, covering topics such as Machine Learning, Natural Language Processing, Computer Vision, and AI Ethics.

- Part 1 contemplates concepts starting with the letters A to D.
- Part 2 contemplates concepts initiated by the letters E to M.
- Part 3 contemplates concepts starting with the letters N to Z.

15.15   Prompt Engineering - Volumes 1 to 6.

This collection covers all the fundamentals of prompt engineering, providing a complete foundation for professional development.

With a rich variety of prompts for areas such as leadership, digital marketing, and information technology, it offers practical examples to improve clarity, decision-making, and gain valuable insights.

The volumes cover the following subjects:

- Volume 1: Fundamentals. Structuring Concepts and History of Prompt Engineering.

- Volume 2: Tools and Technologies, State and Context Management, and Ethics and Security.
- Volume 3: Language Models, Tokenization, and Training Methods.
- Volume 4: How to Ask Right Questions.
- Volume 5: Case Studies and Errors.
- Volume 6: The Best Prompts.

15.16   Guide to Being a Prompt Engineer – Volumes 1 and 2.

The collection explores the advanced fundamentals and skills required to be a successful prompt engineer, highlighting the benefits, risks, and the critical role this role plays in the development of artificial intelligence.

Volume 1 covers crafting effective prompts, while Volume 2 is a guide to understanding and applying the fundamentals of Prompt Engineering.

15.17   Data Governance with AI – Volumes 1 to 3.

Find out how to implement effective data governance with this comprehensive collection. Offering practical guidance, this collection covers everything from data architecture and organization to protection and quality assurance, providing a complete view to transform data into strategic assets.

Volume 1 addresses practices and regulations. Volume 2 explores in depth the processes, techniques, and best practices for conducting effective audits on data models. Volume 3 is your definitive guide to deploying data governance with AI.

## 15.18 Algorithm Governance.

This book looks at the impact of algorithms on society, exploring their foundations and addressing ethical and regulatory issues. It addresses transparency, accountability, and bias, with practical solutions for auditing and monitoring algorithms in sectors such as finance, health, and education.

## 15.19 From IT Professional to AI Expert: The Ultimate Guide to a Successful Career Transition.

For Information Technology professionals, the transition to AI represents a unique opportunity to enhance skills and contribute to the development of innovative solutions that shape the future.

In this book, we investigate the reasons for making this transition, the essential skills, the best learning path, and the prospects for the future of the IT job market.

## 15.20 Intelligent Leadership with AI: Transform Your Team and Drive Results.

This book reveals how artificial intelligence can revolutionize team management and maximize organizational performance.

By combining traditional leadership techniques with AI-powered insights, such as predictive analytics-based leadership, you'll learn how to optimize processes, make more strategic decisions, and create more efficient and engaged teams.

## 15.21 Impacts and Transformations: Complete Collection.

This collection offers a comprehensive and multifaceted analysis of the transformations brought about by Artificial Intelligence in contemporary society.

- Volume 1: Challenges and Solutions in the Detection of Texts Generated by Artificial Intelligence.
- Volume 2: The Age of Filter Bubbles. Artificial Intelligence and the Illusion of Freedom.
- Volume 3: Content Creation with AI - How to Do It?
- Volume 4: The Singularity Is Closer Than You Think.
- Volume 5: Human Stupidity versus Artificial Intelligence.
- Volume 6: The Age of Stupidity! A Cult of Stupidity?
- Volume 7: Autonomy in Motion: The Intelligent Vehicle Revolution.
- Volume 8: Poiesis and Creativity with AI.
- Volume 9: Perfect Duo: AI + Automation.
- Volume 10: Who Holds the Power of Data?

15.22  Big Data with AI: Complete Collection.

The collection covers everything from the technological fundamentals and architecture of Big Data to the administration and glossary of essential technical terms.

The collection also discusses the future of humanity's relationship with the enormous volume of data generated in the databases of training in Big Data structuring.

- Volume 1: Fundamentals.
- Volume 2: Architecture.
- Volume 3: Implementation.
- Volume 4: Administration.
- Volume 5: Essential Themes and Definitions.
- Volume 6: Data Warehouse, Big Data, and AI.

# 16 About the Author.

I'm Marcus Pinto, better known as Prof. Marcão, a specialist in information technology, information architecture and artificial intelligence.

With more than four decades of dedicated work and research, I have built a solid and recognized trajectory, always focused on making technical knowledge accessible and applicable to all those who seek to understand and stand out in this transformative field.

My experience spans strategic consulting, education and authorship, as well as an extensive performance as an information architecture analyst.

This experience enables me to offer innovative solutions adapted to the constantly evolving needs of the technological market, anticipating trends and creating bridges between technical knowledge and practical impact.

Over the years, I have developed comprehensive and in-depth expertise in data, artificial intelligence, and information governance – areas that have become essential for building robust and secure systems capable of handling the vast volume of data that shapes today's world.

My book collection, available on Amazon, reflects this expertise, addressing topics such as Data Governance, Big Data, and Artificial Intelligence with a clear focus on practical applications and strategic vision.

Author of more than 150 books, I investigate the impact of artificial intelligence in multiple spheres, exploring everything from its technical bases to the ethical issues that become increasingly urgent with the adoption of this technology on a large scale.

In my lectures and mentorships, I share not only the value of AI, but also the challenges and responsibilities that come with its implementation – elements that I consider essential for ethical and conscious adoption.

I believe that technological evolution is an inevitable path. My books are a proposed guide on this path, offering deep and accessible insights for those who want not only to understand, but to master the technologies of the future.

With a focus on education and human development, I invite you to join me on this transformative journey, exploring the possibilities and challenges that this digital age has in store for us.

## 17  How to Contact Prof. Marcão.

17.1    For lectures, training and business mentoring.

marcao.tecno@gmail.com

17.2    Prof. Marcão, on Linkedin.

https://bit.ly/linkedin_profmarcao